RESTAURANT SITE LOCATION

Finding, Negotiating & Securing the Best Food Service Site for Maximum Profit

By Lora Arduser

The Food Service Professionals Guide To:
Finding, Negotiating, & Securing the Best Restaurant Site Location for Maximum Profit:
365 Secrets Revealed

Atlantic Publishing Group, Inc. Copyright © 2003
1210 SW 23rd Place
Ocala, Florida 34474
800-541-1336
352-622-5836 - Fax

www.atlantic-pub.com - Web site
sales@atlantic-pub.com E-mail

SAN Number :268-1250

International Standard Book Number: 0-910627-11-8

Library of Congress Cataloging-in-Publication Data

Arduser, Lora.
Food service professionals guide to. Finding, negotiating & securing the best restaurant site location for maximum profit : 365 secrets revealed / by Lora Arduser.
p. cm.
Includes bibliographical references and index.
ISBN 0-910627-11-8 (pbk. : alk. paper)
I. Title: Finding, negotiating, and securing the best restaurant site location for maximum profit. II. Title.
TX911.3.L62 A74 2002
647.95'068'1--dc21
2002011172

Printed in Canada

CONTENTS

The location of your restaurant can make or break your venture.

INTRODUCTION

Everyone's heard the saying: What are the three most important things when looking for real estate? Location, location, location. While the phrase has almost become a cliché, it is definitely true!

The location you choose for your food service operation can make or break your venture.

Choosing a location is not something that should be done lightly. It is not a difficult task, but finding and securing a location is a process that should involve a significant time investment and a great deal of research. Remember, choosing a poor location is not an easy thing to fix - you can change your marketing plan or your secret sauce recipe, but changing your location is quite a different matter!

Although the location process varies, depending on whether you're looking to expand your existing operation by adding a new establishment, for example, or whether you're searching for your first location, the general principles of location research are the same.

The good news is you've already taken the first step in your research! This manual will help you find the information you need and lead you through the process of *"Finding, Negotiating & Securing the Best Restaurant Site Location for Maximum Profit."*

There are many factors to consider when starting a restaurant.

CHAPTER ONE

KNOW YOURSELF & YOUR MARKET

Your Profile

Before you start looking for the right location for your venture, you should first take an inventory of yourself. Whether you're a seasoned food service professional or someone changing professions to follow your passion, opening a food service establishment can be a daunting task. While there are many factors to consider and a lot of research involved, you should start by researching yourself. Conduct a market study to see if your restaurant concept is feasible:

- **Ask yourself some questions.** The answers to the following questions will help you to determine whether or not you're ready to open a restaurant and have the resources to do it. They will also help you to determine the type of food establishment to pursue if you are undecided. If you are a night owl, for instance, you should not consider opening a breakfast restaurant because of the early morning hours. It's more likely that you'll wake up grumpy and hate going to work every day. The restaurant industry can be tough even if you love it; don't make your work harder by mismatching your concept and your personality. Be realistic.

    - What are your true goals in relation to owning a food service operation?

    - What is your personality? Are you an early riser or a night owl?

- Does your family support this decision and are they prepared to sacrifice their time with you?

- What kind of management experience do you have?

- What kind of restaurant experience do you have?

- How will you finance the operation?

- **Corporate goals.** If you're searching for a location as part of a corporation, use this same strategy to analyze the "personality" and goals of your organization.

  - What type of food do we serve?

  - Who is our typical customer?

  - To what extent do we want to increase our covers?

  - Do we want to expand our target market?

Your Personal Finances

Don't put the cart before the horse. Before you get too far into your search for a restaurant location, take a good, hard look at your finances and determine if you can afford it. This is particularly important if you are a sole proprietor because your personal finances will come into play when you start looking for business financing.

Ask yourself the following basic questions:

- **How is your credit?** To check on your personal credit record, check with one of the three major credit unions:

    Equifax
    www.equifax.com 800-685-1111

    Experian
    www.experian.com....................888-397-3742

    Trans Union
    www.transunion.com 800-888-4213

- **How much of your own money can you afford to tie up in starting your restaurant?** If you're looking for financing, you'll probably have to demonstrate that you are able to finance a portion of your restaurant and/or location purchase yourself. Can you afford the monthly loan payments you'll need to make?

Your Concept

If you're part of an organization looking to expand, you're already selling a concept. However, if you're an individual operator, you'll need to come up with a concept for your restaurant before getting too far into the search for the perfect location. First, consider the following issues:

- **Think about your interests.** If you're going to open a restaurant, you really need to enjoy what you do because it's a 24-hours-a-day, seven-days-a-week job. Are you interested, for example, in a particular type of cuisine? If you adore French food, you aren't going to be happy running a franchise sandwich shop. Do you love to make desserts?

- **Is your chosen concept salable?** While your interests should drive your concept decision, don't forget that whatever your concept is, you are going to have to sell it to the public. Consider whether or not you think customers will be interested in buying the products/services you want to sell. If there is no interest, there is no sale. If there are no sales, there are no profits!

- **Seek a balance between salability and interest.** Keep these two factors in mind. It will allow you to come up with an innovative idea that will also keep you happy in your new location.

- **Develop a mission statement.** If you are still unsure of your concept, take a different approach. Develop a mission statement; this can really help you decide. Your mission statement should tell you what your company's values are, who your customers are, what your economic objectives are, what your goals are, what your products are and what your market is. To develop your mission statement, take a sheet a paper, write down the following headings and fill in each section:
  - Goals
  - Beliefs
  - Values
  - Product
  - Customers
  - Market

- **Use this information to help you channel your thoughts.** Your goals may be "to make a 15 percent profit" or "to establish an upscale breakfast restaurant." Your beliefs could be "to provide quality food at affordable prices." Your customers may be young working couples without children who have a good deal of disposable income. Your market may be "in an urban center" or "in a rural setting." Your mission statement doesn't have to contain much detail at this stage; it is simply a device that will help you to focus on your direction and formulate an idea about the type of location that you're looking for.

Assess Your Marketing Potential - Take a Look at the Competition

Once you've decided upon a concept, focus on determining your potential market. Ask yourself whether your restaurant would be more successful in a largely populated urban area or a quaint rural town. Would it do better in an area where the majority of residents are single or families? What type of customer will purchase your product? How many customers will you need to serve to meet your profit goals?

To know whether or not your idea has marketing potential, you need to be knowledgeable about the restaurant industry. Explore the following:

- **The National Restaurant Association is the leading business association for the restaurant industry.** Membership of the association can give you access to a great deal of information including wage and operations surveys. You can contact the organization by writing to:
  National Restaurant Association
  1200 17th St. NW
  Washington, D.C. 20036
  202-331-5900

- **Visit the National Restaurant Association Web site at www.restaurant.org.** Membership dues are based on your annual sales and the state in which you are located. The association also has regional chapters that you might be interested in joining.

  - **Visit the online magazine *Restaurant USA* at www.restaurant.org/rusa.**

  - **Subscribe to industry trade magazines.** Examples include *Restaurant Hospitality* and *Restaurants and Institutions*. Find these publications on the Web at www.restauranthospitality.com and www.rimag.com. Such publications contain a great deal of information on the industry and can be helpful with everything from coming up with a concept to locating a new dishwasher.

  - **You absolutely need to know your competition.** Find out what other establishments exist in your market. Which ones are marketing the same segment of the population as you? Find out what they are selling and for how much.

  - **Become a "secret shopper."** An easy (and fun) way to find out what the competition is up to is to become a secret shopper. Go to your competitors and eat at their restaurant. Many may even have a carryout menu that you can take with you. Look at the prices and service. How is the food? What does the plate presentation look like? Do they offer anything unique? What is their seating capacity? How is the atmosphere? How busy are they? When are their busy periods?

Network

The restaurant industry is not the easiest industry in which to network, but there are some options. Here are some networking suggestions:

- **Enroll in a culinary program.** Many of the students in a culinary program will be just starting out in the restaurant business, but other students will be entrepreneurs and food service professionals brushing up on their skills. Get to know some of these people. You may even consider forming your own networking group.

- **Join the chamber of commerce.** Joining your local chamber of commerce offers an excellent opportunity for networking and meeting business professionals in the restaurant industry as well as other industries.

- **Visit the local farmers' market.** Established chefs often use area farmers' markets. Strike up a conversation and see if he or she is aware of networking opportunities in the city.

- **Contact your local American Culinary Federation at www.acfchefs.org.**

- **Take the initiative.** Form your own organization! Contact area restaurateurs and see if they would be interested in forming a local organization.

Keep Up with Food Trends

If you're going to own a restaurant, you'll need to keep up with the Joneses. Make sure that you're aware of current food trends. You can't afford to get left behind! Consider the following:

- **Take a look at the *2002 Restaurant Industry Forecast*.** This publication is available from the National Restaurant Association. It will provide you with information on forecasted restaurant industry sales and trends. Currently, industry leaders claim that customers are interested in ethnic menus including Mexican, Southwestern, Asian, Indian, Caribbean and Cajun. The take-out market is interested in lean and healthy menu choices and items made with fresh ingredients and homemade products.

- **Become familiar with your specific segment of the industry.** Along with being generally knowledgeable about the food industry, you need to familiarize yourself about your specific segment of the industry. If, for example, you want to open a pizza restaurant, you'll need to be aware of what makes a pizzeria successful. What marketing works? Who are pizzeria customers? Sections of the industry also have trade publications. For instance, pizzeria owners can find news geared specifically toward pizzerias at www.pizzamarket-place.com.

- **Check with the National Restaurant Association.** Alternatively, do a Web search to locate specific resources for your section of the food industry.

- **Eat out often.** See what other restaurants are doing. What works for them and what doesn't? You can learn from your competitors' successes and mistakes!

- **Subscribe to magazines such as *Gourmet* and *Bon Appetite*.** These magazines are designed for the general public and will help you define current food and dining trends.

- **Don't forget industry magazines.** Magazines such as The American Culinary Federation's *The National Culinary Review* are excellent sources for current food and dining trends as well. The publication is available to members.

Your Customer Profile

Once you have determined the general market that you are looking for, you can focus more closely on the type of customer that you're likely to attract. Are you targeting singles or families? Are you marketing to households with a median income of over $100,000 or under $40,000? This information is important in helping you to narrow down your location choices. If you intend to open a fine-dining establishment, search in neighborhoods where the average household income is high and where people have a good deal of disposable income. If you're opening a fast food franchise, you can locate in a neighborhood that has families with lower incomes. Here are some suggestions on how to gather information that can help you work out your customer profile:

- **Interview potential customers.** Once you have a concept and target market in mind, interview people who would likely be your customers. These people may be friends, or customers at restaurants with a similar theme to the one you want to open. Check with a local grocery store to see if the manager would mind if you interviewed their customers as they exited.

- **Visit similar restaurants.** Dine in restaurants with a similar theme. Who are their customers? How do they market to and service their customers?

- **Talk to restaurant owners.** In general, the restaurant business is a competitive industry, but if you are not in direct competition with a particular restaurant, the owner or manager may be willing to be interviewed and would be an excellent source of information.

- **Trade Magazines.** Trade magazines such as *Restaurant Hospitality* and *Restaurants and Institutions* are good sources for general customer information.

- **National Restaurant Association.** The National Restaurant Association can also provide you with general customer research tips and guidelines.

- **Franchises.** If you're considering opening a franchise, the franchise organization can offer you a wealth of market, competitor and customer information. Also, if you work for a corporation, consult its marketing department. Ask for some promotional material and background company information.

CHAPTER TWO

MARKET RESEARCH

Location Research

When undertaking the task of finding and opening a new restaurant location, it is so important that you don't rush into it. Take your time! Do a great deal of research, and then do some more. The following are the four essential stages of research for finding a location:

- **National research.** This type of research applies mainly to chains or franchise operations. At this stage, you're looking at the entire nation as a prospective market.

- **Market area research.** A market can be a city or a metropolitan statistical area (MSA). (The MSA is a concept used later to discuss census research.) Once you've chosen a suitable city for locating your business, you'll need to explore each potential area of that city. Focus on the one that best reflects your concept and goals.

- **Trade area research.** Trade area refers to the area where you are likely to find most of your customers. For example, you may have defined your market as a suburb called Bevisville. Within that suburb, the majority of your business comes from an area of three blocks. These three blocks are your trade area. While there are no hard-and-fast rules about what percentage of your business makes up a trade area, location experts generally say around 80 percent.

- **Site research.** Finally, you get to look at actual potential sites. At this stage, you will be looking at a few potential sites and comparing characteristics to find the best location for your restaurant.

Detailed Market Research

Depending on your particular situation, you may need to go through all four stages outlined in the "Location Research" section. Alternatively, you may only need to do two or three. It's also important, during the early stages of your search, to carry out some detailed market research regarding the best possible location for your operation. Don't think you can skip this aspect of choosing your restaurant location. Here are some tips:

- **Research sources.** Information can be obtained from various sources; many of these sources will be used at any and all levels of your search. Try, for example, the U.S. Census Bureau. It can provide you with the relevant data at both the national and local levels of your search.

The type of information you are most likely to use includes:

- Population density
- Demographic characteristics of the population (Are they 20-to-40-year-olds? Single homeowners? Families?)
- Information on the competition in the area
- Site characteristics
- Market characteristics
- The amount of money a customer is likely to spend in your operation

Population and Demographics

It's important to know not only how many people are in the area that you are considering, but also their demographic characteristics. If, for example, you're opening a fast food restaurant, your customer profile is going to be very different from the clientele that would patronize a classic French restaurant. While the first may do very well in a particular area, the other may do poorly simply because the population would not support that type of operation. So where do you locate the essential data? Try the following:

- **Essential data.** Concentrate on obtaining the following statistics about the particular areas or cities you are researching:
  - Population
  - Number of households
  - Age groups
  - Income levels
  - Education levels
  - Household size

- **Contact the U.S. Census Bureau.** It can provide you with an excellent source of information on population density statistics as well as population characteristics and general demographics.

- **Online research.** The Census Bureau's Web site is www.census.gov. Three areas on the Census Bureau's Web site of particular interest are: the American Community Survey, Censtats and County Business Patterns.

- **The American Community Survey.** This provides information from the census supplemental survey. This information includes tables with demographic information by county and MSA. As defined by the U.S. Census Bureau, an MSA is an area made up of at least one major city (over 50,000 people) and includes the county or counties located within the MSA. The American Community Survey is a new survey that is replacing the Census Bureau's long survey. It provides economic, social, demographic and housing information for communities every year, instead of every ten years.

- **Censtats.** This gives you the type of economic and demographic information that you can use to compare county by county. The information is updated every two years. This section also includes information on residential building permits that is updated every month.

- **County Business Patterns provides economic information arranged by industry.** Updated every year, County Business Patterns gives you data on the total number of establishments, employment and payroll for over 40,000 zip codes across the country. Metro Business Patterns offers similar data for MSAs.

- **Finally, try to make sure your information is as up to date as possible.** The drawback to much census information is that it is collected only every ten years. If you're looking in an area that has changed a great deal in the last decade, you may want to supplement the information that you obtain from the U.S. Census Bureau with information from demographic research firms. These firms use census data to generate information on population and demographics for areas between census years. Do a Web search to find such firms, or look in your local phone book under "Market Analysis."

Competition

Information on competition may be harder to access than demographics, especially in the competitive restaurant industry. Your best source for information on the competition may be simply to visit and eat at competitors' establishments. Other sources of information on competition include the following:

- **Telephone book.** Get a rough idea of the size of the competition. Take a look at the Yellow Pages. At least you'll get a count and the location of your competitors.

- **Chambers of commerce.** These often keep a list of area businesses. Be careful using this list, however, often it only includes businesses that are members rather than all the businesses in the area.

- **Trade magazines.** These can provide useful sources of competitor information. This is particularly true in the case of regional trade magazines.

- **U.S. Census Bureau.** It holds minimal information on businesses in the area. This information, however, does include the number of businesses and number of employees.

- **Local newspapers.** You can get a sense of the competition from advertisements and job classifieds. Most papers also have a weekly entertainment section that lists a number of the restaurants in town with information on their prices and menus.

- **National Restaurant Association.** The association can provide you with a list, by state, of the number of establishments, projected sales and the number of employees they have at www.restaurant.org/research/forecast_regional.cfm.

Industry Research

Investigate your industry's market research. Again, the National Restaurant Association is a good source for this type of information. Here are some additional ideas:

- **Crest Division's NPD Group.** Consumer Reports on Eating Share Trends (CREST) is an organization that offers information to people in the food industry through NPD Group (www.npd.com) including market information that can prove very useful in your search for a location. This service provides an excellent research tool, but be warned; it can be an expensive option. For more information, contact Cory Fraehsdorf at 847-692-1898 or by e-mail at cory_fraehsdorf@npd.com.

- **Examples of the type of information NPDGroup offers include an annual report on eating patterns in America.** The report is based on daily food and beverage consumption by 5,000 Americans. It can be viewed at Restaurant USA's Web site at www.restaurant.org/rusa/magArticle.cfm?ArticleID=765.

- **Services such as "SalesTrac Weekly."** Available to registered customers, this offers an analysis of restaurant same-store sales by segment and category based on sales obtained from participating chain restaurant operators.

- **Recount.** This service is basically a census for the restaurant industry. It includes over 463,000 restaurants categorized by service type and food specialty. It contains information on target markets and demographics, including information on geography, phone numbers, types of cuisine, estimated sales and employee counts. For example, Recount can tell you the percentages of various styles of restaurants within a particular area. If, for example, you were researching Chicago, it could tell you the breakdown of family-style, hamburger, Asian, Mexican, Italian and pizzeria restaurants.

- **Visit www.marketresearch.com.** This Web site has market research for the restaurant industry available for downloading. Costs run anywhere from $200 to several thousand dollars for reports that include titles such as "Fast Food in the USA," "Dining Out Market Review," "Top Market Share Sandwich" and "Pizza and Chicken Chain Restaurants Survey."

Overview Of Site Characteristics

Determine site characteristics of your restaurant location by visiting and evaluating the potential site. (There are more tips about specific site characteristics in the section "Looking for Your Specific Location.") At this stage, however, all you need to do is consider the following general issues:

- **Market characteristics.** This includes information on local economic conditions, unemployment, population growth or decline and industrial growth or decline. Generally, this information can be gathered from economic development organizations, zoning departments, city building permit departments, area colleges, newspapers, highway departments and local utility companies.

- **Amount of money a customer is likely to spend.** Obtain these figures from the U.S. Department of Labor's Bureau of Labor Statistics' Consumer Expenditure Survey, which can be found at www.bls.gov/cex. The bureau conducts surveys of households in which every household member keeps a list of all their expenditures. This annual survey can give you information on how much money consumers spend on food away from home. The information is presented in several ways including by region, MSA, age, income level and education level.

- **The Census Bureau is yet another good source of this type of information.** The bureau conducts a business survey every five years. Locate these statistics on its Web site, under the business section, entitled Economic Survey.

Who Can Help Narrow the Search?

As you begin researching your location, you'll probably find that you need some help! It's a big undertaking and you should use all the resources available to you. Consider the following:

- **Economic development organizations.** Most states have economic development organizations that can provide you with a wealth of information, such as an overview of the area, the business climate and a list of available sites and buildings. Find a list of such organizations in *Area Development* magazine.

- **Location-finding team.** If you work for a corporation, put together a team of individuals to work on the location process. Select people who have been involved before in locating property. At the same time, try to make the team diverse enough to bring up as many issues or questions as possible. For instance, it would be good to include someone from the production side of the operation as well as the financial side so that the interest of both these groups will be taken into consideration.

- **Sole proprietor.** If you're a sole proprietor, you should also form a "team" to help you with your search. The team may consist simply of you and your partner, or maybe even you and your best friend from college who happens to have a business degree.

- **Map sources.** If you are a member of AAA, you have access to free road maps that will help you in your research. Other map sources include MapBlast, MapQuest and TIGER from the U.S. Census Bureau. TIGER lets you view cities, regions and MSAs. Search for information about census boundaries, highways, MSAs, census tracts, streets, zip codes, family size, household size, percentage of age groups in particular areas, ethnicity and home-ownership rate.

- **Accountant and lawyer.** At some point, your team should include the services of an accountant and a lawyer. You will always need the services of a good accountant and a good lawyer throughout your years as a business owner, so you might as well find people you can trust and bring them on board, early. The expense of their services in the location process will be worth the money they could save you by protecting you from a bad deal.

Other Online Search Possibilities

Of course, some search resources are more expensive than others, but the following list includes many free resources that you can use to help you find the best location for your restaurant. Here are some suggestions for online searches:

- **Search the Web for "economic development organizations."** An example of this type of association can be found at www.pittsyecondev.com.

- *Area Development* **magazine.** *Area Development* is a magazine devoted to site and facility planning. While it appears to be geared more toward industry and manufacturing, it is worth a trip to its Web site at www.areadevelopment.com. Along with looking at site listings, you can also obtain general information about states, such as population figures, leading industries, emerging industries, number of college graduates, taxes and tax incentives.

- **Franchises.** Franchises can provide their prospective owners with a great deal of information to help them with their site search. If you're thinking about buying a franchise, contact your specific franchise to locate these sources. Other general sources on franchises include www.infonews.com/franchise and www.franchise.org.

- **Utility companies.** Utility companies often offer economic development services. These services include community development planning assistance, financial assistance, computerized databases of commercial sites and buildings, site plans, topographic maps, labor demographic information, utility information and community profiles. To view an example of what types of information are available from utility companies, log on to www.cinergy.com.

- **The Census Bureau also offers county block maps and census tract maps.** Geographic Information Systems (GIS) mapping programs are often available through county and city offices. For example, a group of agencies in Cincinnati put together a map program called CAGIS (Cincinnati Area Geographic Information System). This computerized mapping system allows users to view area maps that contain information on land records, sewers, streets, electrical systems and drainage, among other things. These maps are easily accessible through the Internet; you can view them at www.cagis.hamilton-co.org. An Internet search of the area in which you are interested should tell you if this type of map is available in that area.

- **Many companies offer GIS and other mapping services on the Web.** For example, Caliper Corporation, www.caliper.com/mtudinfo.htm, offers a product called Mapitude that can be used for developing maps and other graphics. Geographic Data Technology, www.geographic.com, sells digital street databases and Sites USA, Inc., www.sitesusa.com, offers mapping services, demographics for site analysis and custom store modeling.

- **Try www.bizsites.com/webxtras/locationconsultants.html.** This Web site is an excellent research tool. The site houses a wealth of information. For instance, on this site you can find typical electrical costs for different states, crime rates, labor information, corporate tax rates in each state, a state tax comparison, regional business reviews as well as case studies that will help you learn from other people's mistakes!

- **Other Web sites.** The site www.listsnow.com can provide you with consumer lists and demographics with as much detail as names and phone numbers. Prices vary and can range from $30 to several hundred dollars. This Web site can also provide you with lists of businesses by particular zip codes. These lists include information on type and size, so it would be a good resource when you are assessing the competition. Another site offered by American Business Information is found at www.abii.com. You can set up your own consumer or business demographic list requests. The prices for these lists vary with the amount of information that you are requesting. Prices for information regarding market areas generally range between $2,000 and $4,000.

- **Software packages.** There are software packages that can do market analyses and site analysis. Prices can range anywhere from a couple hundred dollars to a couple of thousand. You can view some software products at www.easidemographics.com. Offered by Easy Analytic Software, Inc., this site also provides some free demographics reports online.

- **Nonprofit organizations.** Many cities and counties have nonprofit economic development groups that also can provide information. Find these by searching on the Internet. An example of one such organization is the Hamilton County Development Company, Inc. at www.hcdc.com.

- **SCORE Association (Service Corps of Retired Executives).** SCORE is a nonprofit association with over 300 chapters in locations throughout the United States. The organization consists of working and retired executives and business owners who donate their time to help new small business owners. This organization offers workshops and free counseling. Contact your local chapter for more information (www.score.org).

Financing and Research

Sometimes, it's a wise move to combine your search for the perfect location with a review of funding possibilities for your new venture. Chances are you'll probably need some form of funding further on down the line, so you might as well start dealing with banks and financial institutions earlier rather than later during the process. They can be a source of information as well as money! Investigate the following possibilities:

- **Chamber of commerce.** Your local chamber of commerce is a good spot for networking. It may also have resources for financing and research.

- **The Beige Book.** This publication includes information gathered by each Federal Reserve Bank on current economic conditions in its district that is displayed in categories such as consumer spending, manufacturing, real estate and construction. Visit www.woodrow.mpls.frb.fed.us/bb/index/html.

- **Small business associations.** Many cities have small business associations. Again, this type of group gives you networking opportunities as well as possible sources of funding. Small business associations often offer loans with low interest rates. Try one of the many publications that are available on the online library at www.sba.gov.

Real Estate Brokers

Real estate agents may best be used when the search has been narrowed to a few communities. Consider the following possibilities:

- **First, check with friends and associates.** Remember, real estate is a word-of-mouth business, and this is often the best avenue for finding a good realtor.

- **Commercial real estate brokers.** Look on the Internet for sources for commercial real estate brokers at www.realtor.com, www.vandema.com or www.anysite.com.

- **Cohen-Esrey is a broker specializing in restaurant sites.** They can be found on the Web at www.cohenesrey.com/restaura.htm. Also, check your area multiple listings service on the Web; they have commercial real estate listings. For example, go to www.cincymls.com.

Selecting a Consultant

You may want to seek the services of a site-finding consultant. This can be an expensive way to narrow your search, so be sure you are clear about exactly what the consultant is being hired to do. This may be a good option for someone looking for a location as an individual. A consultant can give you an unbiased opinion on information and can help you with the legwork. If you decide to hire a location consultant, consider the following issues:

- **Expense.** If you decide to use a consultant, keep in mind that market and location consultants can be expensive. It's worth shopping around and getting references to be sure the consultant that you choose has the necessary experience in the areas that are relevant to your search. Above all, make sure that the consultant has experience in the restaurant industry.

- **Sources for finding consultants.** The choices can be baffling! There are a number of professional organizations you can contact. Try, perhaps, the Independent Real Estate Consultants at www.fastighetsstrategi.se/english, the National Association of Corporate Real Estate Executives at www.nacore.com and the American Management Consultants at www.americanmc.com.

- **Try *Area Development* and other trade magazines.** Also, investigate economic development organizations. These can often be a source of location consultants.

- **Look on the Web specifically for restaurant location consultants**. One such firm, Qualified Solutions Consulting, advertises its services to include market analysis (cost approx. $800), feasibility studies, business plan development, funding, building analysis and recommendation and site planning. Find this group at www.restaurantexperts.com.

- **Decide what you want the consultant to do.** A consultant can do any number of things. Before you hire one, decide how much work you want him or her to undertake. Ask yourself how much work you can afford. A consultant can be given the entire task of choosing a location, or hired specifically to select the general area. If you can afford it, hire him or her to select and evaluate a few communities before you make your final choice.

- **What to do when retaining a location consultant.** Look at more than one consultant and hire the one who best fits your needs. If you're looking in the Midwest, select a consultant that has experience finding locations in that region. When you have targeted a list of potential candidates, request a statement of qualifications, references and a detailed proposal plan.

CHAPTER THREE

HOW TO CONDUCT RESEARCH IN THE GREATER GEOGRAPHIC AREA

Finding Your General Site Location

If you are beginning your location search by looking at the greater geographic area, you will first need to research the general region or state in which you want to locate your business before turning your attention to specific locations. If you work for a corporation or are opening a franchise, you will have an abundance of market information at your fingertips, including what markets make the best location for your type of operation. If, however, you are a sole proprietor, deciding how to pick one area from such a large region can be frightening! Here are some tips on how to help you focus your search at this early stage:

- **Look at your concept.** The concept of your restaurant may dictate the best locations. For example, if you intend to open a southern barbecue carryout, you may do better in the southern part of the U.S. On the other hand, you may do well in the northeast where there is less competition and you could carve out a niche for your restaurant.

- **Look at your personal life.** Take stock. Are you ready to uproot your spouse and kids and take them across the country? While Chicago may be the best location in the world for your concept, it may work just fine in your home state, as well.

- **Go to your local library.** Look at the classifieds in various city newspapers. Look at what types of buildings are offered and at what prices to get an idea if there may be a suitable facility at a suitable price. This will also give you an idea of the cost of living in different areas. If you move, this will be an important factor for your personal life as well as your business life. While you may be able to live on $1,000 a month comfortably in a small southern town, you'll be in trouble in larger cities if you estimate your living needs at the same $1,000 a month.

Setting Up a Database

People look for restaurant locations in many different ways. You may start out looking at the entire country, or you may only be interested in looking at the town in which you currently live. This section offers some basic information about how a database works and why it would be beneficial to you. The following guidelines go through the steps from general to specific; you jump in wherever it fits your situation.

- **Apply your market research data.** Now that you have a general feel for which regions may make sense for your particular concept, begin putting that market research to work! In looking for a restaurant location, the first thing to do is to decide which geographic markets have the demographic characteristics you feel would make your operation successful. After selecting the market area, city or county you feel is the most likely to be successful, focus on neighborhoods and communities within that area to determine the best spot. Finally, after you have selected the community, look for the best specific location for your new restaurant within that community.

- **Organize.** In your research for a restaurant location, you are accumulating a great deal of information. And while the reams of paper you will produce will contain important data, the information itself will be useless unless you figure out a way to organize it. One of the easiest ways is to create a database in a program, such as Microsoft Access. By entering the data into a database, you can view it easily, look at relationships and make some valid decisions regarding your location.

- **The benefits of using a database.** A database has the capacity to keep many separate sets of data in one place and to compare this information. Let's say you decide to create a database for your research. You call this database My Search. Within this database are subsets of information stored as Tables. These subsets, basically, look like spreadsheets. Table 1 could contain information on the population density and demographics of all the cities where you are thinking of locating your new enterprise. Table 2 may contain more specific information on one of the cities at which you are looking. Table 3 may contain the information on a different city. Table 4 could contain information on your competitors in a specific city and Table 5 could contain information on a specific site at which you are looking.

- **Spreadsheets.** If you're not comfortable with database programs, you can also use spreadsheets, like Excel, to organize this data. But, you won't be able to compare information as easily as you would in a database program.

Research Example Using a Database

Although this example can offer only a simplified version of reality, it does give you an idea of how to get started and how to organize and interpret your research material. The information you collect will probably be more detailed, but the same general framework applies. The following is merely a guideline about what type of research information to include in your database:

- **The first piece of information is the customer profile.** What type of customer are you looking for? If you are a franchise or part of a corporation, then you can get the information on important population characteristics from your company or franchise. If you are an individual, you'll need to do industry research yourself or hire someone. Population density is always an important factor and should be included in your research. Your restaurant can't make sales if there are no potential customers in the first place!

- **Demographic characteristics.** Let's say you're opening a pizzeria. Your customer profile and industry research have shown that the demographic characteristics that are important for that type of operation are the age group and family status of the population. The first thing you'll want to do is collect demographic information on the areas at which you are looking. Industry research from the National Restaurant Association shows you that the largest consumers of pizza are families with people in the household between the ages of 25 and 45.

- **Census Bureau data.** For personal reasons, you decide to limit your search to midwestern cities.

You have narrowed your search down to five cities based on your life requirements and the industry research you have done: Cleveland, Louisville, Lexington, Cincinnati, Chicago and Detroit. So, you go to the Census Bureau's Web site and enter the following information into your database table from the Web site for those particular cities. Editor and Publisher (www.editorpublisher.com) also publishes an annual magazine called *Market Guide* that provides updates on population, median income, median age and other basic statistics. This intermediate information can be helpful since the census is only conducted every 10 years.

City	Population	Households	Ages 25-45	Family
Chicago	2,804,506	1,034,979	746,701	624,195
Cincinnati	312,526	145,127	130,305	115,696
Cleveland	463,677	188,120	144,217	202,445
Detroit	901,109	325,078	252,448	202,445
Lexington	456,924	187,391	151,061	118,690
Louisville	680,809	288,010	200,589	190,470

The table shows you the following cities have these percentages of family households:

Chicago 60%

Cincinnati 80%

Detroit..62%

Lexington...63%

Louisville...66%

- **Concentrate on percentages.** It's important that you look at these numbers as percentages so you don't get the wrong impression from the raw numbers. If you just looked at the raw data, for example, you'd see that Chicago has many more households and families than Cincinnati. This does not necessarily mean that Chicago has more households that fit your customer profile than Cincinnati. By changing these numbers into percentages, you are able to make a more valid comparison.

Business Demographics vs. Residential Demographics

Much location and market research is based on households. For businesses like grocery stores, market research based on households makes sense. This is not always the case with market research for restaurants. It is important to make this distinction: When people spend money on food outside of the home, it is not always spent as a household. Consider, for instance, people who go out to lunch at work or teenagers going out with a group of friends. This represents spending on an individual basis. Also, bear in mind the following factors:

- **Look at the tables in the Bureau of Labor Statistics' Consumer Expenditure Survey (www.bls.gov).** Here, information is displayed by reference person (the person filling out the survey) rather than by household. For example, you'll find that as a group, the people surveyed between the ages of 25 and 34 spent $2,309 annually on food away from home during that survey year.

- **How useful is household information?** If your establishment is a family diner, the household may be a valid characteristic for you to look at. If, on the other hand, you run a restaurant serving business-lunch customers, the household is not such a helpful concept.

- **Business-oriented clientele.** If your restaurant is based on customers you receive from the business community, rather than the residential community, you'll need to be more creative regarding which population demographics you focus upon. If you find yourself in this position, a good place to start is with the Economic Census of the Census Bureau. You can search for information on businesses by zip code. Once you find the appropriate zip code or zip codes, you can view information on how many businesses are located within the zip code and how many employees these businesses have. The information is broken into business sectors. If there are factories and retail shops in your zip code, split these out, because factories generally run three shifts. Remember, only one of these shifts would yield likely lunch customers. Retail employees, however, provide a better source of potential customers simply because of retail shops' opening hours.

- **Corroborate your information.** After looking at the census information, you may want to contact your local chamber of commerce and utility company. They will also have some general information on the characteristics of the area's businesses.

Compare population characteristics among neighborhoods.

CHAPTER FOUR

HOW TO CONDUCT RESEARCH IN THE MARKET AREA

Research Your Chosen Neighborhood

Once you've narrowed your search down to a particular city, focus on looking at particular neighborhoods or communities within a city. Compare population characteristics among neighborhoods in order to get a more specific idea of what a location has to offer. Consider the following:

- **Explore zip codes or census tracts.** A census tract is a section of an MSA, usually comprised of 2,500 to 8,000 residents. With reference to the example in the section entitled "Research Example Using a Database," we know that there are many neighborhoods in Cincinnati from which to choose. Decide, therefore, on a specific neighborhood and focus on the finer detail. Go back to the census data, or any other source of information you may have used. Maybe check with economic development organizations, chambers of commerce, planning departments and utility companies.

- **Surveys.** Other important sources of information, at this point in your research, are customer, market and competition surveys.

- **Use a map as a visual aid.** Get a map of the city and have it enlarged. Tack it up on a wall and record the information you are researching on the map. This information will include demographics and customer information, as well as competition location information.

Developing Surveys and Questionnaires

At this level of research, surveys may be more important than the information you collect from census data. Here are some tips about carrying out surveys:

- **Survey types.** When researching a restaurant location, you should conduct three types of surveys after you've selected a market area:
  - Market survey
  - Customer survey
  - Competition survey

- **Formulate questions that are relevant to your particular venture.** The information you acquire from these surveys is only as good as the questions on the survey. If you don't ask the right questions, you won't get data that are useful to you. Therefore, it is very important to take your time and put a lot of thought into the questions on your surveys.

- **Test.** Once you've made your questionnaire, test it out on a friend, family member or colleague. This will help you find any bugs in the survey including questions that don't make sense or may be offensive.

General tips on formulating surveys:

- **Do not make your questions difficult to understand.** This will lead to frustration in your respondent and you will probably get answers that do not always relate to your question.

- **Keep questionnaires short.** People generally get frustrated with answering questionnaires that are overly long. Everyone is busy and the people who answer your survey are doing you a favor; respect the value of their time.

- **Avoid leading questions.** Questions that lead a respondent to a particular answer will not do you any good.

- **Organize you survey into categories.** This will help your interviewee in the answering process. It will also help you to organize your information later.

- **Include a brief introduction in your survey.** State who is conducting the survey and how the information will be used. Tell respondents that their answers will be kept confidential. Because we all get so many telemarketing calls, it is important to establish this up front. In doing so, you are more likely to convince the person to participate in the survey and you are able to gain some of their trust.

- **The first question.** The first question asked on a survey is the most important one. It determines whether or not a person will complete the questionnaire. In order to entice your respondent to continue, make the first question interesting. Try to draw the person in, as a novelist would try to draw in his or her reader.

Market Survey

A market survey is a good tool to use to supplement your census research. Remember, the census is only updated every 10 years. If the area you are considering has undergone a great deal of change in that 10-year period, you'll want to gather some additional information on the demographics of the market. The following is an example of a market survey. The information you need to complete these sheets can usually be found in records at the public library, city offices and the chamber of commerce. Small business associations can also provide you with a wealth of information. A list of Small Business Association home pages listed by state can be found at www.sba.gov/world/states.html.

MARKET SURVEY

Market (City):_____

1. Approximate total population of target market area_____
2. Number of households _____
3. Average household size_____
4. Ages

18-24 ____%		25-34 ____%	
35-50 ____%		51-65 ____%	
over 65 ____%			

5. Annual household income

Below $11,000 ____%		$11,000-24,999 ____%	
$25,000-36,999 ____%		$37,000-49,999 ____%	
$50,000-80,999 ____%		$81,000-$100,000 ____%	
Above $100,000 ____%			

- **Look at your customer profile** to help you decide categories that are appropriate for your market survey.

Customer Surveys

Customer surveys are a good source of information concerning your potential customer. If you are a franchise or part of a corporate identity, this information has probably been researched already. Check with your franchise or company. If you own an existing operation and are expanding or changing locations, use your existing customers to gain this information. If you're opening your first location, however, you will need to accumulate this information in a different way. Consider phone surveys or mailed surveys. If your new location is in a mall or other area with a number of other stores, go to that area and do in-person surveys. Here are some guidelines:

- **In-store surveys.** In-store surveys can be simple or extended. An example of a simple survey would be to have an enlarged map in your entryway. Ask customers where they came from to your restaurant and where they are going when they leave. Use colored pushpins to indicate these spots; red could be where they came from and green could be where they are going. While this survey does not give you a lot of information, it does give you a good idea of your trade area. This information can be extrapolated for use at your new location. Another way to conduct a simple in-store survey is to ask customers for their zip code. You can then use this information with information from the census Web site to construct a customer profile including information such as household size, income level and education.

- **Extended surveys.** Extended surveys will include more information and may look something like the example on the next page.

CUSTOMER SURVEY

What is your favorite cuisine? _____

What are the last three restaurants at which you dined?

1. _____ 2. _____

3. _____

What do you like about this restaurant?

_____

_____

_____

How many people are in your household? ❑ 1 ❑ 2 ❑ 3 ❑ 4+

In what part of town do you live?

_____

_____

How many times a week do you eat out? ❑ 1 ❑ 2 ❑ 3 ❑ 4+

When you dine out, where are you generally coming from and where are you going?

_____

_____

How long would you travel to get to a restaurant?

_____

How much do you spend at restaurants in one week?

_____

_____

- **Afraid customers won't want to take the time to fill out a survey?** Offer a discount on the meal or a free dessert with a completed survey form. The expense will be worth the information you glean!

- **New operators.** What if you are a new individual operator and don't have access to existing customers or corporate data? There are other types of surveys that you could conduct. Investigate the possibilities of using a market research firm to carry out the survey on your behalf. While it can be costly, they do have experience at designing and conducting surveys and may get more usable information than if you go it alone.

- **Politeness.** If you do decide to conduct the survey yourself or with the help of others, be sure that the people doing the survey know exactly what you're looking for and are always courteous to the people they are interviewing.

- **Telephone surveys and in-home surveys.** Telephone surveys are the more inexpensive of the two techniques, but in-home surveys may provide you with more "indirect" information. In the case of the latter, an interviewer can gain a good deal of information from simply noting the neighborhood, size of home and the interviewee's type of car.

- **Be prepared for rejection.** These days you may run into a problem getting people to answer your questionnaire simply because of the number of telemarketing calls people receive. Make it very clear at the beginning that you are not selling anything, you are only conducting a survey. If someone does not want to participate, politely say "thank you" and move on.

- **Incentives.** Offer the interviewee something for their time. Perhaps you could give them a coupon for a free meal when your operation opens.

- **Mailing survey.** Consider renting mailing lists with specific zip codes. If you take this route, make sure that you pay for your respondents' return postage if you want a good response. You can also find mailing list information from www.listsnow.com and www.abii.com. These sites can provide you with mailing or e-mailing lists for your survey.

Competitor Survey

When it comes to assessing the competition, you'd be wise to do some fieldwork. Visit competitors and see what they offer. Using a simple survey, like the example on the following page, can help you track competitor information.

How Many People Should I Survey?

Unfortunately, there is no simple answer to this question. The number of people you survey is partially dependent on the type of survey that you conduct. Consider, however, the following issues:

- **Customer-led surveys.** If you are doing an in-store survey, the number is dependent on how many customers there are. Since you have a captive audience, so to speak, try to get as many customers surveyed as possible.

COMPETITION SURVEY

Competitor Name _____

Location_____

What are the major roads in vicinity? _____

_____

Is there a sign? ❏ yes   ❏ no   How much parking?_____

What are the operating hours? _____

Is it a freestanding building? In a mall?_____

Estimated square footage: _____

What is the general appearance of the building's exterior?

_____

_____

_____

What is the general appearance of the building's interior?

_____

_____

_____

Describe the dining areas (are there booths, tables, type of table-cloths, etc.?): _____

_____

_____

Number of weekly customers: Mon _____   Tues _____

Wed _____   Thurs _____   Fri _____   Sat _____   Sun _____

Do they serve alcohol? ❏ yes   ❏ no

Do they offer carryout? ❏ yes   ❏ no   Delivery? ❏ yes   ❏ no

Catering? ❏ yes   ❏ no

What's the seating capacity? _____

What type of cuisine do they serve? _____

How quickly do they turnover tables? _____

What would you guess the average guest check total is? _____

Do they offer entertainment? ❏ yes   ❏ no

What are the price ranges of appetizers? _____

Entrees?_____ Desserts?_____

- If you are doing an in-home or telephone survey, the rules are different. First, look at the size of the market. If your survey area contains 14,000 people, for instance, you'll want to get a sample that is large enough to reflect the habits of all 14,000, but, at the same time, does not overwhelm your interviewers.

Setting Up a Demographics Database Table

Now that you've gathered more information on the demographics of the potential market area and you have your survey information, you can construct more detailed database tables or spreadsheets to organize the data. Let's continue with our earlier example. From your census information and the market survey that you conducted, you know the following information about each of the market areas that you're considering for your new restaurant:

City	Population	Households	Ages 25-45	Family
Avondale	2,000	750	600	750
Clifton	3,500	1,800	2,400	850
Deer Park	1,500	600	720	500
Downtown	2,000	1,800	1,200	400
Delhi	3,800	1,500	1,400	1,300

The information in this table tells you several things:

- **Avondale:** 30 percent of the population are between 25 and 45 years old and 100 percent of the households are family households.

- **Clifton:** 69 percent of the population is between 25 and 45 years old and 47 percent of the households are family households.

- **Deer Park:** 40 percent of the population is between 25 and 45 years old and 83 percent of the households are family households.

- **Downtown:** 60 percent of the population is between 25 and 45 years old and 22 percent of the households are family households.

- **Delhi:** 37 percent of the population is between 25 and 45 years old and 87 percent of the households are family households.

- **Interpret the data.** From this information one can surmise that Clifton seems to be the best location for both the appropriate age bracket and household composition for your location. Downtown has an advantageous age bracket and Deer Park, Delhi and Avondale all have household compositions that reflect your customer profile.

Setting Up a Customer Survey Database

In addition to the data that you collect from demo-graphics, you can collect other data from your customer surveys. The following table gives you the source of your potential customers. It also provides information about when they eat at your restaurant and where they will be going when they leave. Coupled with the traffic information you gather when you are doing site visits, this information can point you in the direction of a suitable street location. It will even tell you which side of the street would make a better choice! If you decide to locate your restaurant in Avondale, for instance, you'll want to study rush-hour traffic. Which direction are most cars going when 5:00 rush-hour hits? This is the side of the street where you want to locate your restaurant, simply because it provides a convenient stop on the way home.

- **Study the number of times people eat out in a week.** These figures will give you an indication of the sales you can expect to make if you open in that market.

City	Inbound	Outbound	Times Eat Out Wkly
Avondale	Work	Home	5
Clifton	School	Home	6
Deer Park	Home	Home	2
Downtown	Work	Home	5
Delhi	Home	Home	3

- **Customer traffic.** This table shows us where people are going and from where they are coming when they stop at a restaurant in each neighborhood. It also indicates that Avondale, Clifton and Downtown residents eat out the most. These neighborhoods may be better locations than the other neighborhoods based on these variables.

Setting Up a Competitor Database

You need to compile data on potential competitors as well as potential customers. The table that follows shows the number of competitors in each market area, their average size, the average price they make per person on a guest check and their average number of weekly customers. This information will come from your competitor surveys as well as from the fieldwork you have already carried out. Take a look at the following data:

City	# Competitors	Average Size	Average Price	# Weekly Customers
Avondale	4	2,000 sq. ft.	$6.75	250
Clifton	7	2,400 sq. ft.	$8.75	400
Deer Park	3	2,400 sq. ft.	$7.95	310
Downtown	10	1,200 sq. ft.	$10.25	600
Delhi	2	1,800 sq. ft.	$6.75	300

This information offers insight into:
• Potential sales
• Amount of market share you can expect
• General idea of the size of facility you may need

• **The competitors' database also shows you some other interesting information.** Note, for example, that the downtown competitors have less square footage for their stores. This may indicate higher rent and property prices in the downtown area. You can also see that the market in Downtown and Clifton will let you charge more for your menu items.

Neighborhood Demand

One more factor that you should consider is demand. In looking at your community information, you may note that one community has perfect demographics and light competition, but there may simply be no demand for your type of establishment in this area. Here are some tips to help you establish what demand exists for your particular type of restaurant.

- **Per capita expenditure.** In order to figure out demand, calculate what is called the "per capita" expenditure for each community. This information is available through the Bureau of Labor Statistics (www.bls.gov/cex).

- **Annual expenditure.** The tables in the Bureau of Labor Statistics' Consumer Expenditure Survey will tell you how much money is being spent annually by consumers and how much money they are spending annually on food away from home. These tables can present the data by region (midwest, northeast, south and west). You can also find this information for many MSAs on the Web site.

Field Work

Once you have narrowed your search down to one city, you'll want to take some time to get to know the city. What do people's spending habits seem to be like? What is the traffic flow of the city? How does the road system work? The best way to do this is to immerse yourself in the culture of the city. If you already live in the town, you'll already know this information. However, if you are new to the city, you'll do well to spend some time learning the ropes. Here are some tips:

- **Drive, drive, drive.** Drive the city as much as you can. Drive during rush hour, midday, weekends and weekdays. While you're driving, keep your future business hours in mind and pay special attention to these specific times of day. Take a map and a notebook and keep track of how long it takes you to get from place to place.

- **Shop.** Spend time in the area stores. What are people buying? Are there a lot of designer furniture stores but no hardware stores? This may be a signal concerning home-ownership rate and income levels. Pay special attention to the goods in grocery stores. Remember, grocery stores stock items their patrons will buy. In a collegiate neighborhood, for instance, you won't find items packed in bulk. Customers are more likely to buy a single potato rather than five pounds. If you're in an upscale neighborhood grocery store, you're more likely to find health food items and specialty items that you're less likely to find in a more blue-collar neighborhood store. By looking at the goods sold in grocery stores, you can gain some insight into your potential customers and their food preferences.

- **Walk.** While driving gives you one perspective of a city, walking gives you a completely different one. Notice what areas you find people walking in versus the areas that have little foot traffic. If you plan to open an establishment that relies on foot traffic, this is an important step in your research. Plant yourself on a bench and count the number of people that pass during the lunch or dinner hour.

- **Dine.** Eat at as many restaurants as you possibly can. Find out what types of establishments are successful. When are their peak times? What are the most popular items? What are their prices?

- **Economy.** Look at the city's economy. Are there areas in disrepair or areas that seem to be booming? Noticing this type of information will tell you about where to locate a new business as well as how well the city's general economy is doing.

- **Roads and traffic.** How are the areas of the city linked by the road system? Are there major highways or roads that link the various sections and suburbs? Are there barriers to move around, such as rivers or hills?

- **Road networks.** After identifying the types of roads in the city, identify the types of zoning that can be found on them. Once you have located those that seem to be mostly commercially zoned, start watching the traffic patterns. Traffic can be divided into three types: business, living and long distance. What types of traffic are flowing on the roads in the city? Take special note of the traffic that comprises your potential customer base. If you are a destination or special-occasion restaurant, watch long-distance traffic as well as business and local traffic.

CHAPTER FIVE

SALES FORECASTING

Compare and Contrast

Before purchasing a new site, it is important that you produce some detailed sales forecasting figures. You need to know if the new site is capable of generating sufficient sales for you to open and stay in business. An effective method of forecasting is to use comparative information from similar operations, which are generally located in the same or similar area to your potential location. Remember, these establishments also attract the same types of customers. If you are a mid-price diner restaurant, for instance, use other mid-price diner restaurants in the area as a comparison. They don't have to be in the immediate area of your proposed location, but the demographics of their location should be similar. Compare and contrast specific similarities or differences such as physical appearance, size of restaurant, menu and foot traffic. This comparison is a simple matter of research and observation. Try the following approach:

- **Compile a list of the criteria at which you want to look.** Go out and observe these restaurants. Check off how similar or dissimilar they are to your restaurant or proposed restaurant. This will give you the establishments with which to compare sales.

A checklist can be similar to the following simplified version:

Restaurant	1	2	3	4
Size	✓	✓	✓	✓
Menu	✓	✓		✓
Population in area		✓	✓	✓
✓ denotes that the characteristics are similar to those of your proposed site.				

- **Conclusions.** Clearly, Restaurants 2 and 4 are the most similar to your future restaurant. Now you will want to get information on the sales of these restaurants. These sale amounts should be similar to what you can expect.

Rating

Another sales forecasting method is to rate similar establishments and discover those that are the most similar to yours. To use this method, create a table similar to the one above. Ask yourself how much each factor contributes to sales and rate it on a scale from 1 to 10 (1 being the lowest and 10 being the highest), as follows:

Restaurant	1	2	3	4
Size	1	4	10	9
Menu	6	4	1	7
Population in area	8	4	2	6
TOTALS	15	12	13	22

- **From the previous chart, you can draw certain conclusions.** Obviously, Restaurant 4 would be most similar to your future restaurant. But, when rating restaurants to discover potential future sales, you'd be better off making comparisons with more than just one establishment. Establish a cut-off point for what you consider to be "similar" and "dissimilar." For instance, you may decide to look at any comparable restaurant that scores a 15 out of 30 or better.

- **The rating method is different from the "compare-and-contrast" method.** The comparison method leaves you with only a list of restaurants that are similar to yours. The rating method offers greater detail. It also provides information on what factors influence sales.

Forecasting Sales - The Next Stage

If you've used either the "compare and contrast" or the "rating" method to forecast sales, you must now go one step further. Both methods have already identified those establishments that are similar and should, therefore, have similar sales to yours. Now, you need to figure out what those sales are. Bear in mind that it is easier for the potential franchisee than it is for the sole proprietor. If you fall into the latter category, it's not going to be so straightforward to establish potential sales figures. It's very unlikely that you'll walk into a possible competitor's restaurant, introduce yourself as future competition and be given the golden keys to the accounting books! Here are some tips to point you in the right direction:

- **Head count.** Now that you've narrowed down the search and have a list of establishments that are similar to yours, plant yourself outside their front door and count who comes in and out.

- **Investigate further.** Once you have a tally of how many people ate lunch (or breakfast or dinner) at a similar establishment, it's pretty simple to come up with an average of daily sales. But, you'll also need to eat at that restaurant to get the full picture. Get hold of a menu. Figure out the average menu price, then multiply that amount by the number of people that day.

- **Take a look at the following example:** A bistro around the corner from the location you've been eyeing sells six lunch entrees for $6.75, $7.25, $8.50, $9.50, $10.50 and $14.75. The average check is estimated at $10. On a Tuesday, between 11:30 a.m. and 1:30 p.m., you count 140 customers. So, an average of how much money it grossed at lunch is around $1,400. While this total doesn't take drinks, appetizers and desserts into account, it is still probably safer to average this way in order to compensate for the customers that may only have ordered low-value items, such as soup or salad.

- **Be warned, however, the above data are meaningless if you only collect them for one day.** Obtain at least a week's worth of counts and remember, Monday is generally a slower day than Saturday. If you have the time, do counts in different seasons to get a more accurate, overall view.

Determining Market Share

Another method you can use to forecast sales for your location is to determine your market share. Market share is the ratio of money spent in your industry within a standard metropolitan area versus your total business sales. Here's how to determine market share:

- **Consumer expenditure.** Figures can be obtained from the U.S. Department of Labor's Bureau of Labor Statistics' Consumer Expenditure Survey, which can be found at www.bls.gov/cex. Another source is the U.S. Department of Commerce's Census of Business, which is conducted every five years (www.doc.gov or www.census.gov). The census includes the Census of Retail Trade and presents information pertaining to the sales, profits and employment of retail companies. Characteristics are presented according to geographic area, type and size of market, merchandise line, SIC (Standard Industrial Classification) code and type and size of company.

Look for the following statistics:
- Population in an MSA
- Dollars spent in the restaurant industry in your MSA
- Number of competitors

- **Example.** You are opening a pizzeria in Louisville. The Bureau of Labor Statistics tells you that there are 680,800 people in Louisville. Each household (a total of 170,200 households) spends an average of $240 a year on restaurants. Household size averages four people. According to the census, there are 200 restaurants in that area. You can now use this information to come up with an estimate of forecasted market share. If this money were split evenly between all the restaurants in Louisville, each restaurant would see $204,240 annually:

$$170,200 \text{ x } \$240 = \$40,848,000 / 200 = \$204,240$$

- **Additional information.** The above information also tells you that you can expect to gross approximately the same amount as these other 200 restaurants. However, keep in mind that because you open a restaurant in the market does not mean that people in Louisville are going to spend an additional $204,240 per year on restaurants. Your part of the market share will include business that comes from existing operations as well as new customers. On the other hand, by opening your business, you may find that consumer expenditures increase slightly. If this is the case, you'll want to strive to pick up and keep this additional business.

- **A word of caution.** Keep in mind that the figures from the Bureau of Labor Statistics are taken at regional level, whereas this Louisville pizzeria example applies them at trade area level. Also, theory and reality are not the same; each restaurant is not going to see the exact same amount in sales. Remember, this is only an estimate that can help you make decisions regarding your restaurant location. It is not a guarantee of your future sales.

Statistical Methods of Sales Forecasting - Creating An Analog Database

A great deal of site selection research includes the use of statistical forecasting models. We will not go into the specifics of these models in this manual, but we will introduce them. We suggest that if you want to use these models as a part of your site search, you should work with a consultant who has expertise in these statistical concepts. Here, however, are the basics:

- **What is an analog database?** This type of database is created from customer, demographic and competitor information. This information is used to determine sales and trade areas. After the information has been entered, correlation and regression techniques are used to determine the relationship between variables. In other words, statistical methods are used to determine how the various items in the database are related to sales. For instance, does driving distance have an impact? The population's education level?

- **Finally, sales of the analog operations are averaged to forecast the sales for your operation.** A word of caution is appropriate in averaging: If all of your database establishments are similar, averaging will work. If, however, you have analog enterprises that vary greatly from most of the others in the database, your average will be skewed and you will want to come up with the mean of the outlying stores to use.

- **Regression method.** This model is basically an equation that relates an operation's sales to specific variables. It is similar to the analog database, but it goes a step further and rates the variables at which you are looking. An advantage of using the regression system in forecasting is that it can break down complicated situations such as the different sets of restaurant customers; breakfast customers, lunch customers and dinner customers.

- **Gravity model.** This method builds a model with which to forecast your restaurant's sales. Rather than using real data, the method creates a model based on the assumption that people tend to gravitate to locations nearest to them. The reasons for choosing a specific restaurant to dine at, however, is often more complicated and distance is not the only factor in customers' decision-making processes. This particular model may work better for a restaurant that is focusing on business lunch customers; customers who only have an hour to get to the restaurant, eat and get back to work. Customers celebrating an occasion at a dinner venue, however, will often travel quite a distance to eat at a special restaurant for the occasion. Advantages of using a gravity model for sales predictions is that it can offer many what-if scenarios and it is good if you are looking at a large market.

Statistical Software Packages and Online Do-It-Yourself Options

There are software statistical packages available, such as SYSTAT, which make it relatively easy for you to manipulate the data correctly and undertake sales forecasting analysis without the assistance of a consultant. Also investigate the following:

- **A variety of statistical software packages are available for purchase at www.spss.com.**

- **Many market research firms will also provide an analysis service.** Check your local Yellow Pages for firms in your area.

- **Online services. Here are a few possibilities:**

    - **CTS: www.cts.com/~ends.** This company offers marketing databases, maps, data analysis and analysis planning.

    - **Claritas: www.claritas.com.** This site provides census-based data and a GIS system that lets you map and analyze a specific geographic area.

- **Magazines.** Magazines such as *American Demographics*, which can be found online at www.inside.com/product/description_amdem.asp, also provide useful market research information.

- **Take a class.** If you have a flair for math, you may want to consider checking into an area community college or online course for statistical classes. It will save you money in the long-term! For online classes, log on to www.ecollege.com.

Knowing your trade area is crucial.

CHAPTER SIX

TRADE AREA CHARACTERISTICS

Location and Trade Area

In establishing a food service facility, the most important location factor is your target market. The distance that your customer will be willing to travel to your venue will depend on your concept. For instance, if you are a country inn, customers will travel a few hours in order to get to this "get-away location." If you are a breakfast spot, however, your customers may only be willing to travel a few minutes from their homes to eat breakfast. Knowing your trade area is crucial in picking a specific location for your restaurant. Once you've completed your customer surveys, you're in a better position to figure out your trade area. If you use the map method, it's very easy. Just draw a line around the majority of the pushpins and you have delineated your trade area. If you have a questionnaire, transpose the information to a map and do the same thing. When drawing the boundaries of your trade area, you will want to keep several additional factors in mind:

- **Competitors.** Find out how many competitors are within your trade area. This can greatly affect your potential sales.

- **Barriers.** Barriers generally refer to physical barriers, such as rivers, mountains and even road construction and traffic patterns. See what type of barriers lie within your trade area. These will affect the likelihood of customers going beyond those barriers to eat at your restaurant.

Labor Costs and Availability

When searching for a location, always keep labor costs and availability in mind, especially if you're doing a larger geographic search for a location. If, for example, you currently work in Dayton, Ohio, and you're thinking of relocating to San Francisco, you'll probably be surprised by the going labor rates of the new city. Investigate the following:

- **There are several sources to check for labor rates.** Check out the U.S. Department of Labor's Web site at www.dol.gov and the Bureau of Labor Statistics at www.bls.gov.

- **State economic development organizations can provide you with wage survey information.** The National Restaurant Association also has wage survey information specifically for the restaurant industry.

- **Labor availability.** In general, there is a shortage of restaurant labor. If you're opening a fine-dining establishment, you'll need to be particularly careful when considering your labor sources. Is there a vocational or culinary school in the area where you could find skilled labor? A good tool for investigating labor availability in particular industries is County Business Patterns, published quarterly by the U.S. Census Bureau. This information is available online at www.census.gov/epcd/cbp/view/cbpview.html. On the site, you can find the number of employees and businesses in a particular county or zip code. You can also compare state and county economic profiles including population, population percentage change from 1990 to 2000, home-ownership rate, households, number of persons per household and much more.

- **Location in relation to product sources.** While this cost is not significant for most establishments located in urban areas, you should factor this in if your establishment is in a rural area, such as a country inn. You might find that you're unable to obtain some products, or you may have to pay higher prices for shipping in more remote locations.

Transportation Costs and Services

In addition to the higher transportation costs for some establishments in more remote areas, you should look into the availability of transportation itself. For instance, do your vendors' trucks service that part of the country or that part of the county? Also, look into the following issues:

- **Cost of utilities.** Utility costs can vary greatly. You'd be wise to check into these rates. Check with the local utility companies. Information is available at www.bizsites.com.

- **Zoning.** Zoning laws prohibit certain activities from being conducted in particular areas. For example, a restaurant or a factory can't operate in a part of town that is zoned for residential use. Often mixes are allowed; one area of a county may allow mixed commercial and residential use. Zoning laws also affect elements such as parking, signage, noise and appearance.

- **Parking.** In historic districts, you'll find fairly

heavy restrictions on what type of signage you can use and many laws concerning the appearance of your building, including acceptable remodeling plans.

- **Some cities also restrict the number of particular types of businesses in a certain area.** For instance, these cities may only allow three restaurants in an area. There may be particular commercial areas not zoned for restaurants or there may be ordinances concerning permits, parking or liquor licenses that make a location unusable for you. Do a thorough check with the local zoning office BEFORE you purchase property.

- **Taxes.** Taxes will probably not make or break your location decision, but you should be aware of the state and city taxes for which you will be responsible before entering into a location deal. You will want to know about property taxes as well and you may need to find out about corporation taxes. Check with the city tax department for information. You can also get information on various state tax rates at www.bizsites.com.

Trade Area Characteristics

Trade areas are usually divided into three zones: the core (comprised of 50 percent or more of your customers), the secondary zone (comprised of about 25 percent of your customers) and the tertiary zone (comprised of about 10 percent of your customers). Trade areas also fall into particular zones that are classified according to the part of town they fall in:

- **Downtown.** Trade areas in a downtown area reflect the geometric layout of most downtown streets. If you're considering locating your restaurant in a downtown area, look at all the businesses, department and other retail stores, entertainment venues and government offices. A simple count of these types of activities, as well as a count of your competitors, will help you determine the amount of business you can expect. Noting their locations will help you determine a location for your restaurant. If there is a thriving theater district, it would help your dinner restaurant's sales if you were located in close proximity. People tend to walk only a few blocks to get to restaurants, especially if they don't want to miss the opening curtain! Also, take note of how much parking there is and where lots are located. Most downtown restaurants do not have their own lots, but you may be able to take advantage of a nearby public parking lot.

- **Note the major routes in and out of the downtown area.** Many people come to work in downtown areas from the suburbs. Locating your operation along or near one of these routes could be beneficial. In many cities, especially larger ones, people use public transportation more than their own. If this is the case in the city you're looking at, then familiarize yourself with the public transportation routes and schedules, before picking a location.

- **Downtown population.** Find out how many people live in the downtown area. Check your demographic sources to find out how many people reside in the downtown area; this could have an impact on your sales.

- **Urban.** The urban area surrounds the central business district of a downtown area. Generally there are older buildings and you may find factories and railroads as well as older homes in such an area. These areas are usually the ones that city planners focus on for development. While it might not sound like an appealing location at first glance, explore the option of locating your restaurant in such an area if redevelopment is underway. In Cincinnati, for example, this area is known as Over the Rhine. In the last ten years, many restaurants, bars and artists' studios have moved into the area forming their own little entertainment district. If you're looking for an older building (and the historic tax credit that could go along with it), these areas are excellent areas on which to focus your search.

- **Suburban.** Suburban areas have really become their own little downtowns. They have all their own services, including restaurants, so there isn't a need for residents to leave for anything. If you look at suburbs for a possible restaurant location, you'll find that buildings are newer than the ones in downtown areas and generally offer better parking facilities.

- **Rural.** If you decide to open your restaurant in a rural location, you will not draw as many customers because there are fewer residents. The best establishments to thrive in a rural location are those that are destination spots. If you want to open a country inn, a rural location is excellent. If you're opening a fairly normal lunch restaurant, you'll probably only draw from the limited population that lives in the area. Before you look at the actual site, you need to do the same research on the trade area as you did for the larger geographic region.

- **Demographics.** First, determine the population density and demographics of the trade area. Again, contact the U.S. Census Bureau for this information. Look for information by census tract. The local planning department is a good source for population estimates. The post office can also provide you with some information by zip code. Aerial photographs can give you a visual idea of population density. For demographic information, visit the Census Bureau's Web site and www.bizsites.com. Also, check with local chambers of commerce or local market analysis research firms.

- **Competition.** Shop the competition in the trade area. Plot these competitors on a map and make a table similar to the table you created for competitors in your market area.

You may want to consider leasing rather than buying.

CHAPTER SEVEN

LOOKING FOR
YOUR SPECIFIC LOCATION

Lease vs. Own

You may wish to consider leasing rather than buying a location for your restaurant. Generally, leasing a building involves less expense up front. Also, there may be certain tax advantages to leasing. Additionally, if the time ever comes when you want to move on, it is easier to do so. You also avoid the costly selling process. If you decide to go for a commercial lease, look at the following:

- **Length of lease.** Many commercial leases run for five or ten years rather than a single year.

- **Rent and rent increase.** Investigate whether the rent includes insurance, property taxes and maintenance costs (called a gross lease) or whether you will be charged for these items separately (called a net lease).

- **The security deposit and conditions for its return.**

- **The square footage of the space you are renting.**

- **How improvements and modifications will be handled.** Who, for example, will pay for them?

- **Who will maintain and repair the premises?**

- **Whether there's an option to renew the lease.** Or, possibly expand the space at a later date.

- **How the lease may be terminated.** This includes notice requirements and penalties for early termination.

- **Whether disputes must be mediated or arbitrated as an alternative to court.**

- **Commercial leases are different from residential leases.** Commercial leases do not fall under most consumer protection laws. For example, there are no caps on security deposits or rules protecting a tenant's privacy. Commercial leases are usually customized to the landlord's needs. But, they can also be subject to much more negotiation between business owners and the landlord as well. Because there is no standard format, be sure to carefully read each lease agreement you consider. Unlike residential leases where if you break the lease you simply forfeit your security deposit, commercial leases are contracts. If you break such a contract, more than your security deposit may be at stake.

- **Think before you enter into a lease agreement** and make sure it fits your business needs now and in the future. Consider where you think your business will be in the future if you're entering into a long-term lease agreement. Make sure the lease covers your ability to make the necessary modifications your building may need now or five years down the road.

- **Make sure you are able to put up a sign.** If you're leasing in a large commercial complex, make sure the lease includes some competition safeguards for you. You don't want to open your coffee shop and see the landlord rent the space next door to another coffee shop two months later!

- **Consider engaging a leasing broker** to help you locate business leases. Leasing brokers work much the same way as real estate brokers. They will do a lot of the legwork for a fee.

- **Have a lawyer review any lease before you sign it.**

Franchise

If you're uncertain as to the type of operation you want to own, you may want to look into franchise opportunities. Basically, a franchise allows you to buy an existing business with an existing system in place for a fee. For this fee, which typically can run several thousand dollars, you get the right to use the company's name and you get assistance from the franchiser in setting up and running your business. This assistance can include finding a location, training and marketing advice. Consider the following:

- **By buying a franchise, you can limit up-front costs in buying a business.** But, bear in mind that you're also required to give up some control because you will be obligated to follow the franchiser's rules.

- **If you are opening a restaurant because you love to be creative, a franchise is not the best option for you.** If, however, you know little about the restaurant industry and you are simply looking for a business, it may be a good option.

- **Don't forget that many of the costs you incur if you take on a franchise are similar to those you incur if you open your own independent business.** These costs include such things as rental/location purchase costs, equipment costs, operating costs and insurance. You may also incur the following additional costs to the franchiser: initial fee, grand opening fee, royalty fees and advertising fees.

- **Examples of franchises include Subways and Penn Stations.** The Web site www.franchiseopportunities.com can link you to franchise opportunities across the country. Check your local paper as well; franchise opportunities are often listed in the classified section.

- **Franchiser control.** Because all franchises are operating under the same name, the franchiser will want to have some control and be sure that the customer is getting a consistent product and consistent service at every franchise location. Some controls franchisers may have in place include:
  - Site approval
  - Site design or appearance standards
  - Periodic renovations or seasonal design changes
  - Restrictions on goods and services offered for sale
  - Pre-approved signs
  - Employee uniforms
  - Fixed advertisements
  - Particular accounting or bookkeeping procedures

- Purchasing supplies from approved suppliers only
- Limiting your business to a specific territory

- **Keep in mind that franchise contracts are for a limited time,** usually 15 to 20 years. When that time is up, you usually are not guaranteed renewal on your franchise license.

- **Franchise advice.** To help you evaluate whether owning a franchise is right for you, the Federal Trade Commission has a booklet and online information regarding purchasing a franchise business. You can reach them at 877-FTC-HELP or www.ftc.gov.

- **Several states also regulate the sale of franchises.** Check with your state Division of Securities or Office of Attorney General for more information.

Existing Operation

There are also numerous opportunities for buying existing operations. Points to consider include:

- **Buying an existing operation requires less capital at the start of your venture.** This is because, in many cases, when someone sells an existing operation, the transaction includes all the equipment as well.

- **You need to be extremely careful if you're considering buying an existing operation.** You don't want to buy one that is a failing business. Take a look at the company's financial records over the past several years to get a clear indication of the company's financial health. While you may be able to breathe some life back into the business, don't expect miracles.

- **Do some sleuthing.** Find out why the seller is selling and what the word on the street is about the location.

- **Be on site for a few days and see what happens at the operation—now.** Make sure the location is a good one for your operation.

- **Find existing operations for sale in the classified section of newspapers.** Also, try trade publications.

New Buildings vs. Existing Buildings

There are pros and cons to both new and existing buildings. Review the differences carefully to determine what will work best for your restaurant.

- **New buildings.** The good thing about new buildings is that you shouldn't have to carry out lengthy renovations, remodeling or updating before you can start operating.

- **New buildings will also be up to code.**

- **If you're buying a site to buy a structure, you may find this Web address useful: www.CMDFirstSource.com/means/index.asp.** After registering as a user, you can enter information on the type of structure you want to build, the gross square feet you need and the zip code. The program will then provide you with an itemized cost estimate. You can find a database for building codes for most major cities on this same Web site.

- **Existing buildings.** Older buildings often have more character than new buildings.

- **You may be able to benefit from a tax break with some older buildings.** Since 1976 there have been provisions in the federal tax code to benefit taxpayers who own historic commercial buildings. These buildings are structures that are listed on the National Register of Historic Places or are in national historic districts or local historic districts or are National Historic Landmarks. This tax credit has gone a long way towards helping cities revitalize historic areas. Currently the tax benefit to the owner is a 20 percent tax credit. For further information on this tax credit, visit the Internal Revenue Service's Web site at www.irs.gov, or write to: Federal Historic Preservation Tax Incentives, Heritage Preservation Services (2255), National Park Service, 1849 C St. NW, Washington, D.C. 20240. They can be reached by email at hps-info@nps.gov or by phone at 202-343-9594.

Location Requirements

You will need to consider whether or not you want the restaurant to be a freestanding structure or part of a strip mall or shopping center. Consider the advantages and disadvantages of each type of location. Will tourists be a significant part of your business? You may want to consider locating in a theme/historical shopping area such as Albuquerque's Old Town. On the other hand, many popular family-owned Mexican restaurants are located in strip malls in Albuquerque. Here are some additional considerations:

- **Freestanding location.** Freestanding locations have their good and bad points. For example, if you're located in such a facility, you may not have the benefit of business created by nearby stores. On the other hand, you do have more flexibility with how you use your space. You also have greater scope for expansion compared with operations in a mall or part of a strip mall. Further, you don't have to worry about regulations that might govern what type of sign you can use. And, you don't have to share your parking space!

- **If you choose to be part of a shopping area, you're likely to attract customers from the other business areas.** However, there may also be more competition in such an area compared with a freestanding location. You may also find more space and parking constraints in a shopping area location.

- **Consider whether or not to locate in the urban center or the suburbs of the community.** Does your customer profile tell you your customers will be lunching business people? If so, you'll do better in the urban center where more businesses are likely to be located.

Strip Mall Locations

If you decide to locate in a strip mall, there are three positions your restaurant can be in: detached from the other buildings, attached to the other stores in the strip mall and at one end of a line of attached buildings. Here are some tips for choosing the best strip mall location for your operation:

- **Freestanding.** In general, the freestanding building may be the best and most visible option.

- **Attached.** Of all the attached premises, the ones at the ends produce more sales than those in the middle. Usually, also, one end of the strip mall has higher visibility.

- **The middle stores in a strip mall are more problematic.** When you are housed in one of these you become one of the crowd and it's hard for the potential customer to notice you. On top of this, many lessors will have restrictions on signage, so you may not be able to differentiate yourself with your restaurant's sign. There may be other ways to distinguish yourself, however, depending on your lease agreement. Put tables outside or a sandwich board listing specials. Consider using piped-out music to attract customers. Or, put one of your servers on the sidewalk with samples.

- **If your restaurant is located right in the center, you may have greater visibility due to the architecture of the building.** Be sure to pay attention to any anchor stores, such as major department stores, in the mall. You will have higher visibility located next to such buildings.

- **Finally, if you decide to locate in a strip mall location, pay attention to other shopping venues in the area.** Generally, where there is one strip mall, there is another. Be sure that you're not locating your restaurant in a secondary location. Pay attention to how visible your location will be to someone driving by. Can they pick you out of all the other options they are seeing?

- **Find out from the owner if there are plans to build in the lots in front of your strip mall**, thus obscuring your future visibility.

- **Think about where you want to take your operation in the future.** If you're planning to expand in five years, a strip mall location may not be the best choice because it could limit, or eliminate, your expansion plans.

Shopping Mall Locations

If you decide to look at shopping mall locations, you'll also want to do your homework. Visit the mall and find out what stores are already there and what new stores are planned. Investigate the potential:

- **Square footage.** Find out what you can about available square footage and the going rates.

- **Pay attention to peak shopping hours.** Also note the customer mix.

- **Location of major stores.** As in the strip mall location, make a note of where the larger stores, such as department stores, are located. A location near one of these gives you an advantage.

- **Stay away from dead-end corridors.** Customers tend to avoid exploring in a mall if they don't see much activity down the corridor.

- **Many of the malls nowadays have food courts.** Consider locating your restaurant in one of these.

Be aware, however, that this will limit what you can do. Operations in food courts are typically small, so you may have to serve a limited menu due to the space and equipment constraints. Naturally, this may affect your sales and ability to make profits.

Facility Requirements

You also need to think about space and design requirements for your site. Break up the operation between front of the house and back of the house and figure out what you need in both areas:

- **According to facility experts, dining will take up the majority of your space.** This is followed by kitchen and prep space and then by storage space. Usually, space breaks down as follows:

  - 40-60 percent of total facility for dining space
  - Approximately 30 percent for kitchen
  - About 12 percent should be for actual food preparation, with the remainder being production space allocated to dishwashing, trash and receiving, etc.
  - Storage and administrative office make up the remainder of the total available space

- **Design consultant.** If you're starting from scratch, you may want to engage the services of an architect or restaurant design consultant. But, be warned; the services of these professionals can cost several thousand dollars.

- **How much room do you need for dining?** Your sales forecast information can provide you with some information on how much dining space you will need. Let's say your sales forecast tells you that you have the potential to make $20,000 a week serving 800 people. You plan to be open six days a week and you estimate you can turn your tables once a night, so you need to be able to fit approximately 70 patrons at a time (800 people/6 days = 133.33 people; 133.33 people/2 table turns = 66.66). For dining you will need about 15-18 square feet per customer per table. Therefore, you will need approximately 1,300 square feet for dining. Remember, this doesn't take the bar, lobby, hostess area, coatroom or restrooms into consideration.

- **If you have a bar, you should have about one bar seat for every three dining seats.** Allow two square feet for bar stools and chairs and about 10-12 square feet per customer at a table.

Examples of Space Requirements

Here are the typical space requirements of a few types of food service operations to help you:

- **Pizzeria.** For the production area in a neighborhood pizzeria, you'll need room for a steam table, a cold food table, pizza ovens, sandwich ovens and a fryer. If it's a carryout establishment, you'll need a counter and cash register for the front area. If you serve customers at the facility, you will also need a dining area, customer restrooms and maybe room for a jukebox and a place for coats. Most pizzerias don't have an abundance of seating because they are designed primarily as carryout and/or home-delivery operations. For these you need between 800 and 1,500 square feet. For a larger facility with a dining area, about 2,500 to 4,000 square feet is necessary.

- **Sandwich shop.** You will probably need between 500 and 3,000 square feet.

- **Coffeehouse.** You'll need between 800 and 3,000 square feet.

- **Bakery.** If your customers do not eat at the facility, you can get away with 1,000 to 1,500 square feet. If they do eat on the premises, you'll want up to 3,000 square feet.

Site Characteristics

Now that you have picked the community in which you wish to locate your restaurant and you've decided on the type of facility that will work for you, you must pick the specific site. What are the elements of a successful location for your operation? In a restaurant, the most important factor is whether you can you draw in the customers. Specific site characteristics, above all other factors, have greater influence upon deciding the success of your operation. Let's say you've narrowed your search down to three locations in the neighborhood of Clifton in Cincinnati to open your pizzeria. Now you need to compare these locations to determine which one is the best. Here are some crucial factors you need to consider:

- **Visibility.** How easy is it for the customer to see the location? You'll get maximum visibility if you are located on the far corner of a main road inter-secting a secondary road.

- **You should also try to find a level location.** This will enhance your visibility and it will help make it easier for drivers to get in and out of your parking lot, particularly in the winter when there many be ice and snow.

- **Try to avoid dead-end and one-way streets.**

- **Parking.** How much parking is there? The Urban Land Institute (www.uli.org) and International Council of Shopping Centers (www.icsc.org) lists standard ratios of parking needed for shopping centers. They suggest that there should be at least 2.2 square feet of parking for every square foot of shopping center space. For supermarkets they suggest at least three square feet of parking for every square foot of supermarket space. In areas with little parking or areas with higher crime rates, you may want to consider using valet parking.

- **Ingress/egress.** How easy is it to get into the parking lot and leave the parking lot? Look at the roads in front of a possible location. Are there medians? These can make turning into your parking lot a problem.

- **What about traffic lights?** If you are on a busy road and your site is located on a corner without a light, customers may find it difficult to access your restaurant.

- **Accessibility.** How easy is it for your customers to get to the location from their homes and/or businesses? One of the things you'll want to do is drive the trade area. Get in your car and drive from various points to your possible location. How long does it take you to get there? If you're going to be serving lunch, drive during the lunch hour. Serving dinner? How long does it take to get to the location during rush hour?

- **Retail synergy.** How does the presence or absence of other retailers affect consumer traffic? When we use the word "competition," it usually has a negative connotation, but not all other business is competition. Synergism refers to the idea that you can increase business because of your proximity of other businesses. Now, you probably won't experience synergism if you're a French restaurant located beside another French restaurant. But, if you're a French restaurant and there is a steak house, a Japanese restaurant, a furniture store and a shopping mall on the same block, you'll probably see increased sales because of the increased exposure you're gaining to potential customers. Fast food restaurants seem to be an exception to the synergism rule; the fact that another fast food restaurant is near by doesn't appear to impact sales negatively.

- **Security.** How safe is the location perceived to be? Check with the local police department to see what types for problems have gone on in the neighborhood. Be sure to make your specific site safe with outside lighting as well.

Site Visit

Now that you've made a list of the site characteristics that are important for your operation, take this list with you when you conduct site visits at your potential locations. Make a worksheet you can use to compare the sites on which you are focusing:

Take a look at the following examples:

Site address: 3217 Jefferson, Cincinnati, OH 45219

	Visibility	Parking	Ingress	Access	Synergy	Security
Excellent		✓				✓
Good	✓					
Average				✓	✓	
Poor			✓			

Comments: *Building is new, looks like little remodeling to be done.*

Site address: 316 Ludlow, Cincinnati, OH 45220

	Visibility	Parking	Ingress	Access	Synergy	Security
Excellent		✓			✓	
Good	✓					
Average			✓	✓		✓
Poor						

Comments: *Building was a flower shop, will need remodeling.*

Site address: 16 Corry St., Cincinnati, OH 45219

	Visibility	Parking	Ingress	Access	Synergy	Security
Excellent	✓				✓	✓
Good			✓			
Average				✓		
Poor		✓				

Comments: *Seller flexible on price due to poor parking situation.*

- **Now, put all this information into a database or spreadsheet application.** This enables you to compare factors easily.

ADDRESS:	3217 Jefferson	316 Ludlow	16 Corry
Visibility	Good	Good	Excellent
Parking	Excellent	Excellent	Poor
Ingress	Poor	Average	Good
Accessibility	Average	Average	Average
Synergy	Average	Excellent	Excellent
Security	Excellent	Average	Excellent

- **In reality, no site will be 100 percent perfect.** You're probably going to have to make some tough decisions at this point of your search. Look at the example above. None of these are perfect choices, so now you need to take a hard look at which of these factors are the most important to the success of your future restaurant. Let's continue with our pizzeria example from earlier. Let's say we are looking at a college neighborhood and we plan to offer carryout and delivery service. With this in mind, a site with good security (since our drivers will be carrying cash), good parking and good ingress will be important. Of the three sites, 316 Ludlow will probably be our best choice, looking at this information. Using the information gathered from the site visits described in the previous chapter, investigate further:

- **Compare cost per square footage.** You can obtain square footage measurements from your realtor, the multiple listing services and the county auditor's Web page.

- Let's set up another table for square foot measurements and cost:

ADDRESS:	3217 Jefferson	316 Ludlow	16 Corry
Selling Price	$85,000	$120,000	$175,000
Square Feet	2,400	3,000	3,800
Cost Per Square Foot	$35.42	$40.00	$46.05

- **Check with your realtor about the average cost per square foot in the area.** Compare this with your table so that you don't overpay!

- **Don't worry about lack of access.** If you don't have access to the building you're interested in, you can still gather some information about it regarding size and required improvements.

- **Sanborn Fire Insurance Maps.** These maps were created for insurance underwriters who used them to determine risks and establish premiums. Today, however, these maps tend to be used mainly by researchers into history, urban geography, architectural history and preservation. Access these maps at www.sanborn.umi.com. You can also check with your local library or historical society. These maps can provide you with information on building size and layout and could be particularly helpful if you're looking at locations where you don't have access to the building to do any measuring for yourself.

- **Auditors' Web site.** Many of the county auditor offices have Web sites that you can use to look up information about specific properties. By searching the address, you can obtain information about building size, price of the sale, former owners and improvements. Most of these will include information on commercial buildings as well as residential ones. For example, visit the Hamilton County Ohio Web site at www.hamiltoncountyauditor.org.

- **Neighborhood.** Take a look at the neighborhood of the proposed location. How old is it? Is the neighborhood in decline or is there new construction going on? Notice if there are many vacant lots and properties for sale. Are there parks, schools, businesses, hospitals, places of entertainment such as movie theaters or ballparks? All of these factors can be a detriment or a plus to you depending upon your chosen type of operation.

- **Demographics.** Just as with your larger search, neighborhood demographics are an important research tool. Who lives and works in your neighborhood? Are there enough people in the neighborhood that fit your customer profile to make your restaurant profitable?

Traffic Count

At this point in your search, you can do a traffic count to analyze the number of potential customers. This is going to mean camping out at your potential location and simply counting cars. Make a sheet to help you. See the next page for an example.

- **Peak hours.** By recording the number of cars that pass each hour you can easily get an idea of the number of potential customers. It will also enable you to identify peak driving hours. If you're opening a restaurant and plan to serve lunch and dinner, you will want to find a location that has peak traffic hours between 1 a.m. and 2 p.m. and again between 5 p.m. and 7 or 8 p.m.

TRAFFIC COUNT FOR LOCATION 1

Hour Ending	Number of Cars
10 a.m.	
11 a.m.	
12 p.m.	
1 p.m.	
2 p.m.	
3 p.m.	
4 p.m.	
5 p.m.	
6 p.m.	
7 p.m.	
8 p.m.	
9 p.m.	
10 p.m.	
11 p.m.	

- **Accessibility.** Along with doing a traffic count, you'll need to determine how much hassle it would be for customers to get to this particular site. How much traffic will a potential customer have to fight to get there? Is the site on a one-way road making parking a possible difficulty? Some of this information you can get from driving the area yourself. Other information you can obtain from your customer surveys.

Competition

Look at the direct competition. It's one of the best ways to determine what share of the trade area you require in order to ensure profitability. Divide the number of competitors into the population of the trade area. This will give you an indication of your anticipated market share. For instance, the trade area has a population of 5,000. There are 10 other pizzerias in the trade area, so you would need 500 customers to be successful in this area. Here are some tips for sizing up the competition:

- **Make an inventory.** Construct this inventory by referring to the phone book. Drive round the area and make notes on competitors.

- **Check area coupon books**. Many restaurants are listed in local coupon books.

- **Once you've completed your inventory, locate each of your "rivals" on your wall map.** It will give you an overall view of what the competition looks like.

- **Categorize competitors.** Place each of these competitors into one of two categories: direct or indirect competition. The direct competitors' category refers to restaurants with the same concept. In this case, it would be all the pizzerias. Indirect competitors are all the other restaurants – they all sell food, but they do not offer your particular menu type.

- **Rate sales impact of competitors.** Finally, rate the sales impact that the competitors would have on your restaurant. One way to achieve this is to work out the distance the competitors are from your location. Also, consider whether the competition is in a position to intercept customers.

- **The close proximity factor.** If it becomes clear that distance is an important variable in your sales forecasting, you could plot the competitors on the map and assess whether or not their position would be advantageous for intercepting customers who could be on their way to your location. If the competition happens to be very close to your location, then it might seriously impact upon your sales.

- **Other factors.** If distance is not an important factor in your sales forecasting, you'll need to turn your attention to whatever other factors may be relevant and rate your competitors accordingly. For example, if your restaurant is a unique dining concept and attracts customers simply for its unparalleled menu, take a very close look at your competitors' menus. In this case, you'd probably find that your target market is spread across a larger area.

- **Take a look at this example of the competition.** Let's say the establishments in the table on the next page represent all the restaurants in your trade area. By recording this information and placing it in a database, you can easily compare your direct and indirect competition. The information will help you determine the size of facility that you need and the weekly sales income you can expect from your new establishment.

- **Optimum space.** You can see from the table that your direct competitors are using 750 and 8,000 square feet of space. It is probably safe to assume you will need a facility in a similar size range. If you anticipate higher sales like Pablito's, or even one of your indirect competitors, look for a larger building.

Name	Direct/ Indirect	Location	Size (sq. ft)	Weekly Sales
Pablito's	D	5th & 3rd	8,000	$30,000
Bob's Steakhouse	I	1600 Blue St.	7,500	$25,000
Joe's Surf and Turf	I	16 N Third	8,000	$15,000
Angie's Pizza	D	Main & 6th	750	$5,500
The Corner Shop	I	1414 Corner	1,000	$8,500
Teri's Bar and Grill	I	12 11th	1,050	$10,000

The commercial buying process has several steps.

CHAPTER EIGHT

SECURING AND NEGOTIATING A LOCATION

Feasibility Study

The process of buying a commercial location is very much like securing real estate for your home. You'll make an offer on the property, then you have to go through financing, inspections, appraisals and permitting. So far, we've devoted a lot of attention to how to find the perfect spot. Now we'll look at what you need to do once you've found that spot. Long before you get to the point of hiring a real estate agent, you'll want to conduct a feasibility study and write a business plan. Here's how to proceed:

- **What is a feasibility study?** A feasibility study looks at your business and analyzes its ability to be successful and profitable. A feasibility study can help pull all this information together.

- **Necessary information.** When developing your feasibility study, you need information concerning costs such as linen, employee uniforms, equipment, china, insurance, utility bills, rent or mortgage, office supplies, payroll expenses, taxes, advertising expenses, repair and maintenance expenses, food cost, wages, health insurance and workmens' compensation expenses. This information, along with your projected sales information, will help you draw a good picture of your restaurant's potential health and help you determine what prices you'll need to charge to remain in operation - at a profit. **101**

- **Contact the National Restaurant Association.** It has sample feasibility studies that may be helpful in creating your own. To obtain information on feasibility studies, membership, or other issues, visit their Web site at www.restaurant.org or write to National Restaurant Association, 1200 17th St. NW, Washington, D.C., 20036, 202-331-5960

Developing a Business Plan

Every business needs to have a business, or strategic, plan in place. It helps you keep your goals in focus. A business plan is basically a written statement that guides you in your business. In addition, if you are searching for financing for your operation, most banks and lenders require a business plan before making a loan. When you look for a restaurant location, we can pretty much assume you'll need to get financing, especially if it involves buying a piece of property. The following tips will help you develop a business plan:

- **A great source for a pre-written business plan for restaurants is Quickplan** located at www.atlantic-pub.com.

A business plan contains the following components:

- **Cover letter.** The cover letter includes the name, address and telephone number of the business and the names of all principals.

- **Statement of purpose.** This can be a relatively short statement and be taken from the mission statement you developed at the beginning of your location search.

- **Table of contents.** Make sure to include a table of

contents so your reader will be able to find sections easily. The easier your business plan is to read, the less frustrated your loan officer will be and, in general, it's easier to work with a happy loan officer!

- **Application and expected effect of loan.** The application is something you can get from the lending institution. Be sure to include the purpose for your loan. If you're buying a franchise, spell out the costs that are involved. If you're building a new structure, include information on all your cost estimates. If you're buying an existing building, you may need to include information on remodeling costs.

- **Description of the business.** In this section, state your goals. Detail why you want to go into business and what you hope to achieve. This section should also provide a detailed description of your business. You can get the terminology and style for this section from thinking about your restaurant concept. Also, in this section, you'll need to describe your business, your product (your menu) and the location in which you wish to open your restaurant. In the business description you need to include information such as whether you are a sole proprietor, corporation or partnership. Will the business be a franchise or an independent business? Also, talk about the potential for your restaurant to be profitable and to grow. State when you intend to open the restaurant for business and describe any unique features or menu items.

- **Description of product.** In this section, describe your menu. What kind of food and service does it entail? Is your type of restaurant in demand? What is unique about your restaurant or menu?

- **Location description.** Describe where your restaurant will be located. Include information such as visibility and square footage. For a real estate loan, you will want to make this as detailed as possible and include information on how the location will help make your business profitable.

- **Management.** In the beginning this may only include you. If you have key people lined up for certain positions (including yourself), provide information on these people including a resume. What are their skills and how will they help the business make money so that you can keep up with your loan payments? You will also need to include costs for management's monthly salaries.

- **Personnel.** For this section, you should include information on how much labor it will take to run your restaurant. You won't have names, but list these by position. How many grill cooks will you need? Bartenders? Servers? Also, provide information on what you expect to have to pay these employees. You can put the information into a table similar to the following:

Employee	Pay Rate per Hour	Hours per Shift	Total
Lunch server	$3.15	4	$12.60
Lunch server	$3.15	4	$12.60
Lunch server	$3.15	4	$12.60
Lunch grill cook	$10.00	6	$60.00
Lunch fry cook	$9.00	6	$54.00
Lunch dishwasher	$7.50	8	$60.00
Lunch host	$8.00	4	$32.00
Lunch bartender	$9.50	4	$38.00
Assistant manager	$12.00	8	$96.00
TOTAL LUNCH SALARIES			**$377.80**

- **Of course you will need to carry this computation further than just one shift**; you will need to illustrate how much labor the restaurant will require on a monthly basis.

- **Competition.** This section should include information on three to five of your nearest direct competitors. Also, who are your indirect competitors? How are their businesses doing? What are their strengths and weaknesses and how is your operation different from theirs?

- **Pricing and sales.** This section should contain information on how you plan to price your menu items. If you have an existing operation, this part of the business plan will be easy. If you are a new restaurant operator, this section will take some more work. First, before determining the prices of your menu items, you'll have to have a clear idea of what your menu will look like and what items you intend to sell. To do this, you'll need to go back to your concept and customer profile. Let's say that your concept is the pizzeria. Your customer profile tells you your customers want a more upscale, gourmet pizzeria. Taking this information into consideration, you decide to create the following menu template:

  - **Vegetarian Delight** – artichokes, Roma tomatoes, black olives and goat cheese on a thin wood-fired crust with pesto sauce
  - **Spinach Lover's** – spinach, sun-dried tomatoes, Fontina and feta cheese and red onion on a wood-fired crust drizzled with roasted garlic olive oil
  - **The Unregular** – spicy Mariana sauce topped with tapenade, portabella mushrooms, proscuitto and smoked provolone

- **I'm Stuffed** – a double decker pizza filled with eggplant, Mariana, provolone and hot Italian sausage

- **Note that the menu items fit with the market research you have conducted.** But, you'll still have to come up with a price. Now you need to do some research with area suppliers. Determine the prices of the ingredients so you can cost out each menu item. After collecting supplier information, you find that the items on your menu will have the following food costs:
  - Vegetarian Delight - $2.50
  - Spinach Lover's - $3.25
  - The Unregular - $3.25
  - I'm Stuffed - $2.85

- **Now you need to determine the labor for each item.** Let's say that most items in your new restaurant have comparable labor costs. Looking at the labor figures you researched for your trade area, you know that your kitchen staff will be making between $8 and $10 an hour. You have experimented with making the pizzas and know that each pizza takes about 10 minutes to make. Therefore, the labor cost per pizza will be $1.50 (we took the average labor cost of $9 and divided it into 60 minutes).

- **How do you calculate your overhead cost?** Take it from your business plan. Your business plan should take into account everything you will be spending in overhead. Calculate your daily overhead costs, then look at your sale forecasts. Let's say that your daily overhead is projected to be $400. Your projected sales forecast is $1,200. (You got this from looking at your competitors' sales.) You also found that your competitors served about 200 people daily; therefore, the overhead cost per customer is $0.50. Your pizzas serve four people, so the overhead cost per pizza is $2. Now, add your food, labor and overhead costs. For The Unregular, these costs would be: $3.25 + $1.50 + $2 = $6.75.

Now, look at your business plan and see how much you are allotted for profit. Let's say it is 15 percent of your sales. Therefore, the cost of the Unregular pizza will be $6.75 + $1 (15 percent of $6.75) = $7.75.

Marketing Plan — An Important Part of the Business Plan

Use your customer profile and demographic research to create a marketing plan. This section should describe your typical customer, define your target market, how you intend to advertise and promote your business and your pricing strategy. It will also include thoughts on the likelihood of growth and expansion. If you are part of a corporation or a franchise, the marketing plan is often laid out for you. If you're going into business independently, you'll want to think of creative, inexpensive ways to advertise that you're now open for business. You probably won't be able to afford television or radio time immediately, so think of other avenues to create sales:

• **Donate food to a local public radio fund drive.** This will give you free advertising on the station when they thank the people who donated food.

• **Visit your local chamber of commerce.** All cities have festivals, parades and other events. See how you can involve your restaurant.

- **Set up cooking demonstrations at a local mall.**

- **Hold a grand opening event.**

- **Whichever way you decide to market yourself, include this information in your business plan.** This is important so that the lending institution can see that you have ideas on how to market and sell your product.

Management Plan — An Important Part of the Business Plan

Owning a restaurant means managing. You have to manage the operation, the finances and the employees. A strong management plan will help you develop policies and goals to make your restaurant a success. If you are lacking in financial or people-management skills, describe in this section how you intend to rectify this. You may consider taking some classes yourself or hiring people qualified to take care of these aspects of the business. Your management plan should also include how your background/business experience helps you, what your weaknesses are and how you can overcome them, the members of the management team and their duties, policies for hiring and training, wage and benefits policies and employee policies.

- **Sales projections.** Take your sales projections from the earlier research that you conducted. The form on the following page gives you an example of how you might present your sales forecast:

	Daily	**Weekly**	**Annually**
No. of Seats			
No. of Meals Served			
Average Check			
Total Food Sales			
Total Food Cost			
Gross Profit			
EXPENSES			
Labor			
Overhead			
Total Net Profit			

- **Financial management plan.** You need to present a realistic budget in this section. Accurately determine the actual amount of money needed to open your restaurant and how much you need for daily operating costs. There are two different types of budgets: a start-up budget and an operating budget. To create a start-up budget, you need to account for one-time costs such as your site/location purchase, major equipment, utility deposits, down payments, legal/professional fees, licenses/permits, equipment, menu production cost and insurance. Your operating budget should include how much it will take to keep your restaurant running for three to six months. This budget should include insurance, rent, depreciation, loan payments, food cost, advertising/promotions, legal/accounting, payroll expenses, salaries/wages, utilities, taxes and repairs/maintenance.

- A useful resource to help you calculate operating expenses can be found on the National Restaurant

Association's Web page at www.restaurant.org/ research/ _ratios.cfm. This page gives you operating statistics for full service and limited service restaurants. The numbers are expressed as a percentage of total sales. For instance, for a full-service restaurant with guest checks that average less than $10, you can expect to spend 28 percent of your total sales on food, 30 percent on salaries, 5 percent on employee benefits and 6 percent on occupancy costs. The information in this report is part of the 2002 Restaurant Industry Operations Survey. This survey is issued annually. If you take part in the survey, the National Restaurant Association will give you a copy of the National Restaurant Association's Restaurant Industry Operations Report. This includes information on cost of sales, gross profit and utility expenses.

- **You may want to get the help and advice of an accountant at this point in time.** Making sure your financial statements are in order is a crucial step in securing a loan. SCORE is also a good resource for financial statement planning. Another very useful resource is the Uniform System of Accounts for Restaurants. This book provides information on record keeping systems for restaurants. It is available through the National Restaurant Association's online bookstore for about $30 for members.

- **Financial statements.** The main component of the financial segment of your business plan is the balance sheet, the statement of cash flows and the income statement. If you are a new business, you won't have a history of financial statements to show to a bank or other investors for your sales track record. The business plan does this for you. If you're just starting a restaurant, base these statements on your sales forecasts. Obtain this information from the statement of cash flows. If you're an existing business and you are looking to move your restaurant's location, or you're expanding to a new location, your past financial statements are an important component of your search for new financing.

- **Income statement.** This statement, also known as a profit and loss statement, is based on your sales forecast figures. To these figures, you then add information on how much it will cost to run the business. Include the following information: net sales, cost of sales, operating expenses, operating profit, taxes on income and net income. An example of an income statement follows:

PROFIT AND LOSS FORECAST
Sales
Costs
Payroll
Food Cost
Benefits
Advertising
Utilities
Maintenance
Mortgage (or Rent)
Insurance
Property taxes
Total Costs
Income Before Taxes
Taxes
Income After Taxes

- **Balance sheet.** A balance sheet is an itemized list of total assets and liabilities of the business showing the business's net worth. A sample follows:

ASSETS	LIABILITIES
Current	Current
Cash	Taxes owed
Accounts receivable	Salaries owed
Inventory	Loans
Supplies	Accounts payable
TOTAL CURRENT ASSETS	**TOTAL CURRENT LIABILITIES**
Fixed	Long-term
Real estate	Term loans
Fixtures	Mortgage
Equipment	**TOTAL LONG-TERM LIABILITIES**
Vehicles	
TOTAL FIXED ASSETS	
TOTAL ASSETS	**TOTAL LIABILITIES**
NET WORTH	

- **Statement of cash flows.** This statement shows net income and gives a bank an idea of the likelihood of the business being able to pay its debts. In general, the statement of cash flows works the same way as your checking account. When you receive money, you record it in your checkbook and when you pay a bill you subtract that amount from your checkbook. When you open a business, you should remember that revenue comes in slower than the bills. So, you don't want to incur more expenses than necessary at the start-up stage. Here's an example of a statement of cash flows sheet:

	Before Opening	Monthly Operations	Yearly Operations
Sources of Cash			
Personal Assets			
Loans			
Food Sales			
TOTAL			
Use of Cash			
Purchasing Property			
Operating Expenses			
Food Cost			
Payroll			
Insurance			
Taxes			
Utilities			
Advertising			
Maintenance			
Furniture			
Equipment			
TOTAL			
CASH FLOW			

- **Purchase a combination form that makes it easier for your loan officer to read.** Contact The Risk Management Associates, One Liberty Place, 1650 Market Street, Suite 2300, Philadelphia, PA 19103, 800-677-7621. Their Web address is: www.rmahq.org.

Creating Your Own Business Plan

If you decide to prepare your own financial statements but you don't have a particularly strong business background, it would be a good idea to have an accountant review these forms before you go to the bank for a loan:

- **Breakeven analysis.** This analysis helps you figure out the sales level you must reach based on your forecasted sales. An accountant could help you develop this section of your business plan since it isn't as straightforward as the other sections of the business plan.

- **Capital equipment list.** This list should include your major equipment rather than equipment that is frequently replaced, such as china. This list should include walk-ins, steam tables, slicers, work tables, fryers, grills, ranges, dishwashers and sinks. It should also include major dining room furniture and bar equipment. Also, include the cost of each piece of equipment on this list.

- **Supporting documents.** Supporting documents include items such as resumés for you and key management, your credit report, copies of leases, copies of contracts and anything else relevant to your restaurant business plan.

- **Sources of funding.** You need to include information on where you expect to get your funding. If family is investing, include that in this section. If you have partners, include information on how much funding is to be derived from this source. You also need to include any funding from yourself.

Business Plan Resources

Your business plan is a very important document for two reasons: it helps you to focus on what your goals are and it helps to secure financing. There are many sources to consult when writing your business plan. This is an extremely important document for your business so don't just wing it; get some expert advice and use it!

- **Small Business Administration (SBA).** The SBA offers a "Resource Directory for Small Business Management" which includes a wealth of information, including how to write business plans. For a free copy, contact your nearest SBA office or log on to www.sba.gov.

- **Service Corps of Retired Executives** (SCORE) offers workshops and free counseling.

- **Business Information Centers** (BICs) offer resources and on-site counseling for businesses. For more information about SBA business development programs and services, call the SBA Small Business Answer Desk at 800-U-ASK-SBA (800-827-5722) or log on to www.sba.gov/bi/bics.

- **U.S. Government Resources.** The Government Printing Office (GPO) offers resources to business owners as well. GPO bookstores are located in 24 major cities and listed in the Yellow Pages under the "bookstore" heading. You can write to Government Printing Office, Superintendent of Documents, Washington, D.C. 20402-9328 to request a list of materials that they publish or you can also purchase items from the bookstore online at http://bookstore.gpo.gov.

- **U.S. Department of Treasury Internal Revenue Service (IRS).** The IRS offers information on tax requirements for small businesses. You can write to them at P.O. Box 25866, Richmond, VA 23260, or call 800-424-3676.

- **The National Restaurant Association.** The National Restaurant Association also has publications that can help you write a business plan. You can purchase these at a discounted price if you are a member.

CHAPTER NINE

START-UP MONEY

Funding Sources

Start-up money can be generated from a variety of sources. Investigate the following possibilities:

- **Yourself.** Inventory your assets, including real property, retirement funds, vehicles, savings accounts, stock funds and other investments. You may elect to use some of these assets as cash, or you may be able to use them for loan collateral. While you need to be sure you don't strap yourself, it's always good to use at least some of your own money to start your restaurant. By not borrowing the full amount, your loan payments will be smaller and you may enhance your ability to borrow in the future, should you need to.

- **Family and friends.** While it may be good advice to "never loan a friend money," many businesses have been started on just such a loan. This area can be very sticky, however. Make sure you put everything in writing to protect both parties.

- **Traditional loans.** Banks will lend money to new businesses, but they will ask for collateral. You'll have to be able to offer your house or other assets in order to secure the loan. If you borrow from a bank, you'll need to show them your business plan.

- **Venture capitalist.** Venture capitalists are people who make a living out of investing. Generally, they are not interested in smaller projects, but it may be an avenue you want to pursue.

- **Equity investment.** Equity investment means that you give someone a share of your business for their investment dollars. The investor normally shares in your profits, but only shares in your losses up to the amount of their initial investment. Generally, there are three levels of ownership and investor partnerships: general partner, limited partner and shareholder. A general partner shares in profits and losses in proportion to their investment. This type of partnership generally exists when both parties are willing to work full time in the business. If an investor becomes a limited partner, they do not share in the responsibility of managing the business and their risk is limited to their initial investment. An investor becomes a shareholder if you decide to incorporate your business and sell stock; the investor receives stock shares for his or her investment.

- **The advantages of equity investments.** It may be a good way for you to get the necessary funds to purchase your location and start your business. This may also be a way for you to bring in people who have skills in areas you may lack. However, you should be careful about selling more than 49 percent of your business. If you sell more than half of your business's interest, you also sell your right to make decisions.

Government Programs and Small Business Association Sources

The many government incentives and funding programs available to start in the restaurant trade are well worth exploring. Here are the essentials on several loans available that can be used for start-up and real estate purchases:

- **Check the Catalog of Federal Domestic Assistance.** Visit www.cfda.gov. If you're a member of a minority group, such as a woman-owned business, there may be additional funds available to you. You can access information concerning government grants online at www.sbasmallbusinessloans.com/finnif.htm. This Web page will take you to a secured link where you can purchase access for $49.95.

- **Small Business Association loans.** The government's Small Business Administration program can make direct loans to businesses, but usually they simply guarantee bank loans. To be eligible to be guaranteed by the SBA, your business must be independently owned, must not dominate the field and not exceed their size standards. While there is some flexibility on terms for SBA loans, maximum terms for real estate loans are 25 years. Also, if you're building a structure or carrying out major renovation, the 25-year maximum is in addition to the time needed to complete construction. Interest rates can be negotiated with your SBA lender. But, there are maximums: fixed rate cannot exceed the prime rate (prime + 2.75 percent) if the loan maturity is seven years or more. There are several options for loans through the SBA:

- **SBAExpress & SBALowDoc.** These loan amounts up to $150,000 for up to 25 years.

- **CommunityExpress.** This pilot loan program is designed to stimulate economic development in rural and inner cities. To be eligible for CommunityExpress, small businesses must be part of the SBA's New Markets. These are defined as small businesses owned by minorities, women and veterans who are underrepresented in the population of business owners, compared with their representation in the overall population. The loan also applies to businesses located or locating in low- and moderate-income urban and rural areas. The maximum loan amount is $250,000.

- **Minority Pre-qualification Loan Program and the Women's Pre-qualification Loan Program.** These programs also assist women and minorities in securing business loans. The maximum loan under both of these programs is $250,000.

- **504 Loan Program.** This program, also known as the Certified Development Company Program, provides affordable long-term, fixed-rate loans that can be used for acquiring land and/or buildings. The advantages of the 504 loan over a conventional loan are: a lower down payment, below-market financing and a longer repayment term.

Additional Financing

The SBA, in conjunction with other organizations, also offers financing, other than loans, including:

- **Small Business Investment Companies (SBICs).** SBICs, investment companies licensed by the SBA, put venture capital into small businesses in venture capital investments and long-term loans.

- **Specialized Small Business Investment Companies (SSBICs).** SSBICs make smaller investments than SBICs. They only invest in small businesses owned by socially and economically disadvantaged individuals.

- **The Angel Capital Electronic Network.** This network is a service that gives so-called "angel" investors information on small businesses. More information on these financing opportunities can be found at www.sbasmallbusinessloans.com.

- **Economic Development Administration.** This department of congress makes and guarantees loans to businesses in redevelopment areas. To find out more, visit www.osec.doc.gov/eda.

*Finding a bank
that meets your
needs is crucial.*

CHAPTER TEN

LOANS

Finding a Bank and Banker

Entering into a loan relationship is not something to undertake lightly. Compare it to a marriage rather than a lunch date! Talk to friends and associates. Find out which banks they have dealt with and what experiences they have had with these bankers regarding loans. Bear in mind the following issues:

- **Keep your options open.** If you're locating to a new town and don't know anyone to ask for recommendations, visit several banks. Interview the loan managers. Compare rates, services and customer service. How easy was it to get an appointment with the appropriate person? Did they seem genuinely interested in your business? How well did they explain their services and loan requirements?

- **Keep in mind other factors when you are looking at banks.** It probably makes sense to do your regular banking with the institution through which you receive your business loan. Also, how convenient is this bank and its branches to your location? Do you anticipate doing night drops or needing change throughout the day?

What the Banker Will Want from You

It can be hard to get a commercial loan if you are opening a privately owned small business. If you are a small business, you will find that the banks request a little more from you than is the case with large corporations. In general, corporations are able to negotiate lower rates than small business owners. If you have good credit, however, you may have a little more negotiating power. Whatever your circumstances, the bank will require the following things from you:

- **More financial information.** Banks will ask you for a second and possibly third income source to back up your loan.

- **More collateral.** The general trend is that banks ask for more collateral than they did previously. Nowadays, they may want as much as three times the amount of the loan.

- **Greater ratio of assets to debt**. These days, bankers are looking for you to have three to five times as much equity in your business as you are carrying in loans.

Collateral

If you're applying for a loan, you're going to have to show the loan officer some collateral, or evidence that the bank will be able to collect the money from you - whether you succeed or fail. There are several forms of collateral the bank may be willing to accept:

- **Your signature and credit reputation.** This is called an unsecured loan. It is unlikely, however, that you will find yourself in this type of situation.

Most banks require more than good credit before they will shell out a substantial loan amount.

- **Co-signer.** You may be able to have someone co-sign for your loan. This means that if you can't repay the loan, the co-signer falls responsible. This situation could occur if you had nothing else to offer for collateral. You would want to choose a co-signer who had something to offer, such as real estate or stocks.

- **Real estate.** Real estate, such as your house, is a form of collateral used for long-term loans. You may be able to secure a loan and still keep some of the equity in your home. Check with your loan officer about these options.

- **Savings accounts and certificates of deposit.** These can be signed over to the loaning bank. The account stays open, but you assign the account to the bank and give them your passbook.

- **Cash value of a life insurance policy.** Again, you assign the policy to the loaning bank. You could also borrow against a life insurance policy, but you will probably get a lower interest rate from the bank. So, using it for collateral may be a better option.

- **Stocks and bonds.** Banks will usually lend a percentage of the market value of stocks and bonds in order to account for market fluctuations. The percentage is usually higher on the less-risky stocks and bonds because the latter are subject to less fluctuation.

Negotiating Your Loan

You have on your best suit and you have an excellent business plan in hand. You feel prepared to face the bank, but when you walk through that door, your legs turn to jelly and you feel like you are groveling for any scraps that they might give you. You feel like whatever magic numbers they pull out of their hat, they are the numbers that you have to accept or risk losing the loan altogether. Do you want in on a secret? That isn't true. You need to know the following facts:

- **Loan rates and terms are negotiable.** Up to 60 percent of businesses could get lower rates if they asked rather than just accepted the quoted rates.

- **Loan rates consist of the actual rate and the term (or maturity) of the loan.** Either of these factors may be negotiable.

- **Timing.** The best time to try to negotiate a rate is after the loan officer has made an offer, but before the final papers are drawn.

- **Bankers look at several factors when determining whether or not to approve a loan.** These factors include their assessment of risk (if you are likely to repay the loan), the amount being borrowed and administrative costs.

If you want to ask for a lower interest rate try one of the following strategies:

- **Take a shorter loan period.** The shorter the loan period, the less risk there is to the bank.

- **Improve your collateral.** Again, this helps to eliminate the risk involved with your loan.

Appraisal

As with buying residential property, you'll need to get an appraisal of the property before the loan can go through. Seek the assistance of a local realtor. An agent will be able to provide you with the type of neighborhood, site and market information to which you might not otherwise have had access. Not only can they help negotiate the deal, but realtors can also connect you with appraisers and inspectors that they use and trust:

- **First, contact the local real estate board to find a commercial realtor.** If you begin working with one and you don't like that realtor, get another one. Negotiating your location property is too big a job to leave in the hands of someone you may not like or trust.

- **Your real estate agent can recommend an appraiser.** If you do not use a real estate agent, you can check with your local real estate board or bank for a list of appraisers.

- **Find a listing of brokers and appraisers at www.commercialcentral.com.**

- **Survey and inspections.** A survey and building inspection is obligatory if you're buying an existing building. Even if you're buying a piece of land on which to build, you'll still need to obtain a property survey and instigate a number of environmental inspections. While all these inspections cost money up front, it protects you in the long run. If you have a survey done now, you can avoid problems down the road when you want to expand the parking lot and find out you are pouring asphalt onto the neighbor's property!

- **Don't overlook the fact that inspections may also give you some negotiating leverage.** If inspections turn up some hidden problems, you may have ammunition for lowering the purchase price.

The Deal

If you've never bought real estate before, the closing day can be intimidating. You can expect anything to go wrong - up to the last second. When the signing occurs for a real estate transaction, the people in the room may include you, the seller, both real estate agents, your lawyer, the seller's lawyer and the loan officer. Here are a few tips to help you through the deal process:

- **Take your lawyer with you.** It's important to have your lawyer with you in case there are any last-minute snags. Also, it's reassuring to have someone present who has done this type of deal countless times before. Remember, while it is a routine transaction to the other people in the room, your head is likely to be reeling!

- **The most important rule of all.** Whatever else you do, make sure you get everything in writing!

What If the Deal Breaks Down?

There are many reasons why the deal may break down, but one of the most common is that your financing doesn't go through in time, or for some reason, doesn't go through at all. What do you do if your loan application is rejected?

- **Ask the bank.** Find out specifically why your loan was refused. It may be a simple thing that you can fix. Perhaps you left a key component out of your business plan. If this is the case, rework the plan and go back to the bank. If your credit is the problem, this will take longer to fix. If this is the case, you may end up losing a location. But, get the credit problem straightened out and pursue a new location. Perhaps you don't have enough collateral for the size of loan that you want. Could you make it work with a smaller loan amount?

- **Shop for another bank.** Banks have specific requirements regarding the types of loans they can offer and how many they can approve. It may be that your type of loan or the amount of your loan did not fit into their criteria. If so, shop for another bank.

- **Small Business Administration.** After you have been turned down twice for a loan, you can contact the Small Business Administration. Explore the possibility of obtaining a loan through this organization.

*Various licenses
are needed to serve
food and alcohol.*

CHAPTER ELEVEN

AFTER THE DEAL

Acquiring Licenses and Permits

As a new restaurant operation, you'll also need certain licenses and permits, including:

- **Business license.** In many instances, cities require businesses to have a license. Sometimes you may have to pay a flat fee, other times you may have to pay a percentage of your gross sales.

- **Health department permit.** You will need a license from your county or state health department to cook and sell food. The health department will inspect your operation before issuing the permit and conduct periodic inspections for as long as you stay in business. Inspectors will make sure you are following the law and keeping your food supply safe. They will be interested in food storage, food preparation, cleanliness and installation of equipment, employee cleanliness, restroom cleanliness and the cleaning and storing of equipment. You may incur licensing fees as well.

- **Liquor licenses.** Most states have separate licensing for beer/wine and liquor. Liquor licenses are the more difficult licenses to obtain. In some areas, no new licenses are being issued and you have to buy one from an existing license holder. Beer and wine licenses are usually issued on a yearly basis and are easy to renew, provided your haven't committed any offenses. Check you phone book for the phone number of the local beverage control agency.

- **Fire department permit.** You may be required to obtain a permit from the fire department. Check with your local fire department to see if this applies to your location.

- **Sign permit.** Many areas, especially historic districts, have ordinances regarding what type of signage that businesses can use. If you're in a lease situation, the landlord may also have his or her own requirements.

- **County permit.** Sometimes counties require the same licensure as cities. Check with your county government as well as the city if you're located in an urban area.

- **State licenses.** While food service employees usually do not need state licensure, it is a good idea to check to be sure you are in compliance, especially if you are starting business in a new state and are unfamiliar with their laws.

- **Zoning laws.** Generally, your new location will be located in an area already zoned as commercial. If you construct a new building or undergo extensive remodeling, check local zoning laws first.

Prior to Opening

The deal is closed, your licenses are all in order and here you stand with the keys to your new restaurant. Now what? Now it's time to implement all the ideas in your business plan. But, finally, a few essential matters:

- **Hiring vendors.** It's important that you start contacting vendors before you open your restaurant. You'll need to know what vendors you can use for which products, what days they deliver, what their payment terms are, how you can set up an account and how much lead time you need for placing orders.

- **Hiring staff.** If you're simply moving locations, most of your staff are likely to come with you. If you're opening a new establishment, you will have to find staff. Obvious sources are advertising in the local newspaper. But, you may also want to check any trade schools in the area that have a culinary program. You can also advertise on Web sites such as www.restaurantbeast.com and the National Restaurant Association.

- **Menu.** You've been working on your menu from day one, but now you need to fine tune it. It may be that your newly purchased kitchen allows you to make more "from-scratch" items than you initially thought possible. On the other hand, your prep area may be much smaller than you had anticipated and you may need to make some adjustments to your menu items. You'll also want to fine tune prices. Now that you know what your lease payment or mortgage is, in reality, you may find you need to increase your prices in order to realize your profit goals. If this is the case, you'd be wise to start off with the appropriate prices rather than increase your prices soon after opening. This would only serve to alienate your new customers.

- **Advertising.** You'll want to get the word out about your new location before you open. Take a look at your business plan and follow the plan that you've spent so much time developing. Initially, you'll probably only be involved in out-of-house promotions, but once you open you can also do in-house advertising.

- **Décor and equipment.** Depending on the type of facility you have bought or leased, you may need to update décor and equipment. Or, you may need to purchase new equipment and remodel. The time between signing off on your location deal and opening should be devoted to getting this together. When opening day comes round, you want the place to shine and you certainly don't want a faulty fryer during your first dinner rush!

- **Look at your mission statement again.** You'll also want to take some time to reread and reflect on the mission statement you developed. Now that you have found your location, do you need to make changes to this statement? Once you open, make sure to keep it in a prominent place so that you can constantly be reminded of your goals as a food service operation and a business.

- **Finally - opening your doors.** Congratulations! You are well on your way to a profitable establishment! You have successfully navigated your route to finding the ideal location for your new restaurant. You negotiated the purchase and the financing and here you are ready to open. Now, turn the key, open the door and welcome all your new guests!

INDEX

utilities, 71

V

values, 12
vendors, 133
venture capitalist, 118
visibility, 89

W

wage survey, 70
Web sites, 30
Women's Pre-qualification
     Loan Program, 120

Z

zip codes, 43
zoning, 71
zoning laws, 132

If you enjoyed this book, order the entire series!

Qty	Order Code	Book Title	Price	Total
	Item # RMH-02	THE RESTAURANT MANAGER'S HANDBOOK	$79.95	
	Item # FS1-01	Restaurant Site Location	$19.95	
	Item # FS2-01	Buying & Selling A Restaurant Business	$19.95	
	Item # FS3-01	Restaurant Marketing & Advertising	$19.95	
	Item # FS4-01	Restaurant Promotion & Publicity	$19.95	
	Item # FS5-01	Controlling Operating Costs	$19.95	
	Item # FS6-01	Controlling Food Costs	$19.95	
	Item # FS7-01	Controlling Labor Costs	$19.95	
	Item # FS8-01	Controlling Liquor, Wine & Beverage Costs	$19.95	
	Item # FS9-01	Building Restaurant Profits	$19.95	
	Item # FS10-01	Waiter & Waitress Training	$19.95	
	Item # FS11-01	Bar & Beverage Operation	$19.95	
	Item # FS12-01	Successful Catering	$19.95	
	Item # FS13-01	Food Service Menus	$19.95	
	Item # FS14-01	Restaurant Design	$19.95	
	Item # FS15-01	Increasing Restaurant Sales	$19.95	
	Item # FSALL-01	**Entire 15-Book Series**	**$199.95**	

Best Deal! **SAVE 33%**
All 15 books for $199.95

Subtotal	
Shipping & Handling	
Florida 6% Sales Tax	
TOTAL	

SHIP TO:

Name_____ Phone(____) _____

Company Name_____

Mailing Address _____

City _____ State _____ Zip _____

FAX _____ E-mail _____

❏ My check or money order is enclosed ❏ Please send my order COD ❏ My authorized purchase order is attached

❏ Please charge my: ❏ Mastercard ❏ VISA ❏ American Express ❏ Discover

Card # ☐☐☐☐ – ☐☐☐☐ – ☐☐☐☐ – ☐☐☐☐ Expires ☐☐☐☐

Please make checks payable to: **Atlantic Publishing Company** • 1210 SW 23rd Place • Ocala, FL 34474-7014
USPS Shipping/Handling: add $5.00 first item, and $2.50 each additional or $15.00 for the whole set.
Florida residents PLEASE add the appropriate sales tax for your county.